## FOR THOSE WHO ARE NOT AFRAID TO BELIEVE THE STARTLING TRUTH...

When Clifford Wilson published his great international bestseller, *Crash Go the Chariots,* the world began to see different, more convincing answers to the perplexing questions raised by the strange wonders left behind by the ancients.

Now *The Chariots Still Crash* establishes Clifford Wilson as the Number One authority in this field. From the mysterious landing strips of Peru to the world-view maps of 16th-century Turkey, from the giant statues of Easter Island to the awesome pyramids of Egypt, from Stonehenge in England to the haunting legends of the lost continents, here is the latest, most comprehensive, most illuminating evidence available in the world today!

## THE CHARIOTS STILL CRASH

will amaze you with its startling information about the worlds of scientific super-technology that existed thousands of years ago!

D0957244

# SIGNET Books of Special Interest

# THE CHARIOTS STILL CRASH

## CLIFFORD WILSON

A SIGNET BOOK

NEW AMERICAN LIBRARY

TIMES MIRROR

Copyright © 1975 by Clifford Wilson

SIGNET TRADEMARK REG. U.S. PAT. OFF. AND FOREIGN COUNTRIES
REGISTERED TRADEMARK—MARCA REGISTRADA
HECHO EN CHICAGO, U.S.A.

SIGNET, SIGNET CLASSICS, MENTOR, PLUME AND MERIDIAN BOOKS
are published by The New American Library, Inc.,
1301 Avenue of the Americas, New York, New York 10019

FIRST PRINTING, JANUARY, 1976

  1 2 3 4 5 6 7 8 9

PRINTED IN THE UNITED STATES OF AMERICA

# Contents

# THE
# CHARIOTS
# STILL CRASH

# Introduction

It was my second interview on San Francisco's "Jim Eastman Show"—the previous one had been about eighteen months before.

"Do you still hold to your basic viewpoints in *Crash Go the Chariots,* or have you changed at some points?" Jim asked me.

My answer was that I had learned a lot since writing that book, partly because of letters that had come to me from all around the world, but that "the chariots still crash"—and so a new title was born.

Erich Von Daniken's hypothesis about visits by ancient astronauts who gave their technical assistance in mammoth constructions is quite untenable. This does not rule out UFOs as such, and Von Daniken himself has acknowledged that UFOs as reported all around the world today are not the major subject of his best seller, *Chariots of the Gods?* Despite Von Daniken's theories and speculations, visitors from outer space were *not* responsible for the pyramids, the Easter Island statues, the Piri Re'is map, the so-called electrified ark, the destruction of the cities of Sodom and Gomorrah, or Ezekiel's "space vehicle."

Jim Eastman's question sowed the seed in my mind, and since that time there have been frequent suggestions that there should be a follow-up to *Crash Go the Chariots.* As I have appeared in many television and radio talk shows I have found that the interest in the subject continues, and as questions have been hurled at me I have become more and more convinced that people really are interested in the mysteries of past civilizations.

For reasons entirely beyond this author's control, *Crash Go the Chariots* is, at the time of this writing, virtually unobtainable. Therefore some topics dealt with in that book are looked at again, though not simply to repeat the answers there given. The presentation is deliberately different, and much additional material has been added. Most of the factual material presented is available in technical journals and books on archaeology, but the interpretations are often my own.

*Crash Go the Chariots* was deliberately designed as an answer to Erich Von Daniken's hypothesis: this present book also answers many points he has raised, but its purpose goes considerably beyond that. It is designed as a popular presentation to deal with mysteries of ancient civilizations and achievements. Von Daniken's theories are no more than interesting starting points. We investigate and answer considerably more than he raises about a number of issues.

In this work facts are presented and qualified judgments are given, without undue emphasis on Von Daniken's hypotheses as such. Some may disagree with this new book's conclusions at times, but at least it will be recognized that the foundations are solid and the superstructure is reasonable.

If the response justifies it, it is anticipated that a third volume will follow, for there are intriguing questions on which new light is being thrown by the discoveries of the 1970s. Some of these touch on early civilizations in so-called cradles of civilization; others involve underwater archaeology; yet others involve some of the "established" interpretations centering around recorded history. It is entirely possible that the next decade will see revolutionary changes in some approaches to ancient history, especially as to chronology. Even now, a number of long-held beliefs are being challenged.

The fascinating story continues as the mysteries of

the past are unveiled before us. The certainties of yes-terday are outdated today—the "assured results" of today may be put to one side tomorrow. It is intriguing . . . fascinating. It is *our* past we are looking into, our race, the achievements of our ancestors. It is a privilege, a responsibility—and sometimes a disappointment and a disillusionment—to help unravel the mysteries of the heritage bequeathed to us by our fathers in many lands.

## CHAPTER 1

# No Gold for the Gods

Ecuador could be almost a home away from home for the archaeologist. My first realization of this was after speaking on television in Quito, the capital of that fascinating country.

The session ended, and there were interesting questions and discussions for some time afterward—a common experience when discussing archaeology over radio and TV.

I was about to leave the studio, when I was called back to the telephone. It was a young man from an outer district who insisted he must see me, so I waited for some time until he eventually presented himself. The five minutes I was asked to wait were actually Spanish minutes, but it was worth waiting. He brought with him a number of artifacts, covering no less than three distinct cultural periods of Ecuador's long history. He wanted me to buy them, of course, but that was not all.

*"You must come back and excavate!"*

"Senor, you must come back and excavate—there are wonderful old civilizations here, just waiting for you!"

I listened patiently—and with great interest. However, there was nothing I could do about it, except buy some of his artifacts and ultimately pay for his taxi—I had not realized it was waiting for him at my expense.

This young man was very knowledgeable about the civilizations that had flourished in his own country long ago. However, he certainly did not mention deep caves with metal plates on which the secrets of the uni-

4

verse were inscribed. Nor did he refer to the golden animals about which Erich Von Daniken was to tell an unbelieving world. Nor did any other people in Quito mention them, though some of them discussed their country's archaeological treasures with me at considerable length.

Von Daniken describes these supposed treasures of Ecuador in his third book, *The Gold of the Gods*. If his farfetched claims were true, Ecuador would be swamped by visitors claiming to be archaeologists or anthropologists. The fact is, many of those claims are nonsense. The same pattern of romancing so consistently demonstrated in his first two books is continued in *The Gold of the Gods,* with assertions that cannot be substantiated and "new" discoveries which have the habit of dissipating when investigated.

Once again, the chariots come flaming down, noisily crashing at the center of the earth in mists of distortion and delusion.

## A Vast Network of Underground Vaults?

*The Gold of the Gods* describes a supposed vast network of underground vaults in Ecuador—in the province of Morona-Santiago. Von Daniken claimed that he visited the vaults with their discoverer, Juan Moricz. He tells of seeing a library full of metal plates, many of them gold, and all inscribed with strange writings.

Local people with expertise in geology, mining, and archaeology have no knowledge of the artificial tunnel system, the fabled underground golden zoo, or the library of metal plates—despite their explorations in the designated regions over the past twenty-five years.[1]

To gain his knowledge of *The Gold of the Gods,* Von Daniken found a perfect communicator in the person of Juan Moricz. "He lapped it up," Moricz reported to *Encounter* magazine. Von Daniken was told fantastic tales about caverns and abysses, together with mysterious documents and intriguing adventures. This was something he had wanted for years, for it seemed that at last he had stumbled onto secrets of creation and the very beginnings of the universe.

## A Revealer of Divine Secrets

Despite the fact that he never physically entered the mysterious caves, Von Daniken was soon able to tell of the amazing library he had "seen." Ancient records were inscribed on thousands of sheets of metal, evenly imprinted as though by a machine. They had been written by "a great unknown" for the people of the Space Age.

This interview with Moricz in March, 1972, was a highlight for Von Daniken. Inside the cover of *Chariots of the Gods?* the question is asked in heavy black type, "Was God an Astronaut?" In the same volume Von Daniken talked at length about the so-called sacred books of the world. He also outlined way-out conjectures about the origins of man—Homo sapiens had resulted from an eventually successful breeding experiment between astronauts from space and primitive beings on the earth.

The theme is continued in Von Daniken's second book, first called *Return to the Stars* but later renamed *Gods from Outer Space*. The second chapter of that book is entitled, "On the Track of Life." The author discusses Darwin and evolution, chemistry and biology, RNA and DNA, and he even expounds his views on Genesis 5:1-2 where the biblical story of creation is summarized.

Much of this sort of evidence is scattered throughout Von Daniken's writings, showing that he has an absorbing interest in the origin of life. Now suddenly, unexpectedly, elaborate details are given to him of a metal library, with plates on which all the facts of creation are recorded. Erich Von Daniken saw himself as a great revealer of divine secrets, mysteries toward which the world had been groping through long centuries.

The mere fact that he did not physically see the inscribed sheets of metal was beside the point: the spiritual reality was what counted. This cosmic age was the age of revelation, and Erich Von Daniken was the bearer of the good tidings. His message must be given to the anxiously awaiting world—and so *The Gold of the Gods* was born.

## Prophet of a New Order

In a sense Von Daniken *is* a prophet. Rather subtly, a change has come and the new order has demanded a fresh "revelation." Darwin's theory of evolution had apparently swept all before it, until in the middle of the twentieth century it seemed that only the most gullible of Bible believers continued to accept the Genesis record of special creation. Then came the splitting of the atom, followed by the atomic bomb. Soon schoolboys were being taught that "inside" every atom was a fantastic planetary system, revolving in perfect order, incredible and virtually unexplainable as to "how," but fact nonetheless. Words such as micro-evolution compared with macro-evolution began to be popular.

One consequence was that scientists became increasingly uncomfortable about some aspects of the origin of life, and this discomfort has continued.

The new knowledge about the atom was shattering in some of its implications, and scientists associated with various disciplines have been searching seriously for a new explanation. It has long since been recognized that it is not simply a matter of proceeding from the small to the large, from the simple to the complex, as Darwin had taught: the splitting of the atom had forever destroyed that neat package. Science did not offer a convincing alternative. What was the answer?

History has shown that often there seems to be a

vacuum, and then pseudo-science and cultism take over. Once the vacuum has been created, a new prophet soon emerges. Some members of a gullible public will be waiting to follow the leader, even though it involves the wearing of a mental blindfold.

So it was with Erich Von Daniken and his non-existent metal plates from Ecuador. The scientists and other scholars had failed, but the new messenger now had it all as "assured results," conveniently available only to him on plates which of course no one else could see. The theories of the scholars could be put to one side: the new prophet knew better than the scholars. He now has the answers, answers that may be fantastic, but plausible to those who are eagerly waiting.

Many followers are ready to swallow the weird concoction that is enthusiastically served up to them—at a price, of course. In Von Daniken they see a prophet with a key of knowledge, knowledge that is rejected by the blind and arrogant scholars whose minds are so closed by traditional and "established" schools that they cannot grasp the truth for themselves.

## A Serious Gap Is Filled in

Von Daniken had fulfilled most of the requirements for establishing a new cult, especially by his theories about spacemen breeding with earth-women (or their predecessors). However, there was a serious gap. That seemingly plausible theory, given certain way-out bases, could go only so far. It seemed to answer the question of the origin of Homo sapiens, but this only pushed the problem back one step. Where did the spacemen themselves come from? What was the explanation as to the being behind the spacemen? And what could be known about the origin of life itself?

Von Daniken had rejected the straightforward approach of the Bible. For him it was but one version —the Jewish and Christian accounts—of what had resulted from the counsels of the gods. If only the total picture could be recovered! That had seemed impossible, for why should that revelation be deposited on the little planet Earth? This primitive ball of earth and water, spinning through timeless space, its people backward and lacking in the practice of cosmic principles, could hardly be chosen as the repository for the secrets of the gods.

## An Ancient Switchboard for Electric Contacts?

Then it happened. The new prophet met Juan Moricz in a hotel in Guayaquil, on the seacoast of Ecuador. What more likely place for that depository of the secrets of the gods? As its name implies, Ecuador is crossed by the equator, and visitors from outer space might well choose the center of the earth for their point of contact. Ecuador was actually especially suitable. Pioneer shortwave broadcasting around the world from Quito in Ecuador had proved this. No better site could have been chosen—geological and other factors meant that this seemingly primitive spot at the center of the earth was ideal for radio transmission. Against such an ideal background, Von Daniken asks questions about ancient monsters and Morse code, systems of dots and dashes and SOS's, and a switchboard for electric contacts.[2]

Ecuador, then, was the country to which Erich Von Daniken came and listened entranced as Juan Moricz told his fanciful tales of mystery and adventure. As Von Daniken prodded his willing narrator he heard fantastic story after story about the secrets of the caves and tunnels of this Ecuadorian space-center. It was complete with those mysterious documents, the "cosmic plan" for which Von Daniken had apparently been subconsciously searching for years.

There were of course sinister sentinels who would not lightly give up their secret treasures, guarded so carefully through the centuries—so Von Daniken would have us believe. *Encounter* magazine of August, 1973, reports an interview with Juan Moricz, in which he makes such statements as: "Daniken never set foot in the caves, not unless he did so in a flying saucer. . . . We showed him one of the many cave entrances in the vicinity. You couldn't enter the cave, though, it's blocked." [3]

That *Encounter* article has some discerning comments about the effect of this interview on Von Daniken: "Whatever Daniken may or may not have been fed by Moricz, the fact is that their talk smote him like a revelation. In Moricz, he had for the first time come face to face with a corporeal being who could testify to the activities of extraterrestrial astronauts." [4]

This was the "revelation" that Von Daniken had been groping for, and he now knew that the "cosmic plan," the true story of Creation, had been deposited in this nonexistent library. With this non-information he would be able to completely overthrow the Earth's world order that had proved to be such a failure. He would be in a position to overthrow all known religions.

## Who Took the Photos?

Juan Moricz forthrightly stated in that same article that if Von Daniken claimed he personally saw the library, he was lying—that he had never been shown such things, and that he had even "fiddled the photos," an example being one of Von Daniken's published pictures that was actually taken during an expedition led by Moricz in 1969. At that time Moricz had led a seventeen-man expedition through part of Ecuador's eastern province—they had found stalagmites and stalactites, but no archaeological treasures such as those claimed by Von Daniken. [5]

Moricz went on to acknowledge that he had shown Von Daniken base metal and brass objects in the rear of the Maria Auxiliadora Roman Catholic church in Cuenca, Ecuador. When asked if he had warned Von Daniken that many of the pieces were not authentic, Moricz replied, "Sure, we told him that Crespi [the priest in charge] had collected plenty of valuable stuff at one time, but the genuine pieces are buried under a load of trash. The two rooms are piled high, but most of the contents are junk. Just the same, Daniken insisted on photographing it all. The man's out of his mind. He clicked away from 10 A.M. till 3 P.M., and it wasn't the genuine pieces he illustrated in his book— far from it, in my opinion." [6]

In view of Moricz's statements and Von Daniken's own later admissions, even the first line of Erich Von Daniken's *The Gold of the Gods* is, to say the least, surprising: "To me this is the most incredible, fantastic story of the century."

*"Straight from Science Fiction"*

He goes on to say:

> It could easily have come straight from the realms of Science Fiction if I had not seen and photographed the incredible truth in person.
>
> What I saw was not the product of dreams or imagination, it was real and tangible.
>
> A gigantic system of tunnels . . .[7]

Yes, it is incredible, and it is fantastic. One amazing aspect is that Von Daniken himself eventually acknowledged that he had not been in these tunnels, nor had he been within many miles of them. How could even Erich Von Daniken photograph nonexistent metal plates in tunnels that could not be entered? "He fiddled my photographs of an earlier expedition," Moricz claimed.

Von Daniken leaves no doubt that he is claiming to have entered and investigated the underground tunnels. He says:

During the twenty-four-hour drive to the site we took turns at the wheel. Before we entered the caves, we took the precaution of having a good sleep. When the dawn sky announced the advent of a hot day, our adventure, the biggest in my life, began.[8]

Later he blandly admitted that there had been no twenty-four-hour drive, that he had not entered the caves, and that in various other ways the story should not be taken literally.[9] It is extremely revealing to put his statements acknowledging that he had not been into these tunnels against many other statements in his book:

Birds fluttered past our heads. We felt the draught they created, and shrank back. We switched on our torches and the lamps on our helmets, and there in front of us was the gaping hole which led down into the depths. We slid down a rope to the first platform 250 ft. below the surface. From there we made two further descents of 250 ft. . . .[10]

There are many other points at which Von Daniken makes it clear that he claims to be describing a literal happening—feeling and examining ceilings and walls, laughing as the sound echoed through the tunnels, his doubts about the existence of the underground tunnels vanishing, now able to believe Moricz's story that these tunnels extended for hundreds of miles under the soil of Ecuador and Peru.[11] He describes a skeleton lying at the threshold of a side passage, sprayed all over with gold dust.[12] The huge hall in which he was to eventually see the library measured 153 by 164 yards: "Almost the dimensions of the Pyramid of the Moon at Toetihuacán."[13] He even described a table and seven chairs, the chairs not being made of wood or metal, but of something like plastic, but hard and heavy as steel.[14]

We even read of stone figures into which he bumped at every step.[15]

## Solid Gold Animals?

He described the animals that were there, all made of solid gold—saurians, elephants, lions, crocodiles, jaguars, camels, bears, monkeys, bison, and wolves, with snails and crabs crawling about between all these other animals. He suggests they had been cast in molds, and pointed out that there was no logical sequence about the arrangement—they were not in pairs as with Noah's Ark, nor in species as zoologists would prefer, nor in the hierarchical order that biologists would expect: "The whole thing was like a fantastic zoo, and what is more, all the animals were made of solid gold." [16]

Many of the "solid gold" objects that Von Daniken talks about were made in recent years by local Indians, mainly from metal scraps. The Miami archaeologist Pina Turolla was quoted as stating that the objects were "brass and copper works on display at a church in Cuenca, Ecuador." He said that "natives make the items to swap with a local priest for clothes and a little money." [17] This agrees with the warning given by Juan Moricz concerning the authenticity of the objects in the church—NOT in the unentered tunnels.

## Gold—or Bronze After All?

All this is extremely relevant when we consider Von Daniken's later blithe acknowledgment that he had not been inside the tunnels, and that he did not care whether the animals were gold or bronze. His imagination is certainly brought into full play in this presentation, as when he moves stealthily because "Indians lurk unseen in the undergrowth and watch every movement made by strangers." [18]

He was not even allowed to take photographs as they passed through the tunnels, and we are told that Moricz made all sorts of excuses to prevent him—that the radiation would make the negatives unusable, or that the flash might damage the metal library, and then he "began to sense the reason for Moricz's strange behaviour. You could not get rid of the feeling of being constantly watched, of destroying something magic, of unleashing a catastrophe. Would the entrances suddenly close? Would my flash ignite a synchronised laser beam?" [19]

Then he begged to be allowed to take just one photograph of the pile of gold, and although this permission was refused he was promised that he would be able to photograph plenty of gold later. We then learn "that the biggest gold treasure from the dark tunnels lies in the back patio of the church of Maria Auxiliadora at Cuenca in Ecuador." [20] Von Daniken asks a question that is very easy to answer: "I should like to know what tricks scholars will use to displace this fabulous gold treasure of inestimable archaeological and historical value, which is described here for the first time, from the period in which it does not seem to fit." [21]

"Tricks" are not needed to displace Von Daniken's fabulous gold treasure. The *Encounter* article puts the position neatly: "Daniken is defenceless against his own scheme of things—defenceless, too, against those who seek to exploit, control and delude him with the aid of his own hallucinations." [22]

Gold or no gold, brass or whatever, the amazing Von Daniken assures us that "the minute fraction of the treasure from the patio of the Church of Maria Auxiliadora at Cuenca that I have illustrated here is a still more minute fraction of the precious objects which rest undisturbed in Juan Moricz's tunnels, an orgy of human history in gold." [23]

## "It's Not Really a Zoo"

Questioned about this "golden zoo" that was supposedly in the same chamber as the library, Moricz said that it was not really a zoo, but a faithful representation of plants and animals of the types supposed to have existed centuries before. He added, "What's more, I don't know if they're pure gold—they may only be gilded." [24] Pressed as to where these marvels were, Moricz talked vaguely about an Indian tribe called the Béleas (of whom local people have never heard), and he said his knowledge of the published sheets in the metal library actually came from a guide whom he refused to name. Pressed as to how he knew that these sheets contained a "chronological record of human history," Moricz answered, "I was told so by my guide." [25]

As we have seen, in *The Gold of the Gods* Von Daniken was far more specific than Moricz. He was able to tell about the metal plates, most of whose leaves measured about 3 feet 2 inches by 1 foot 7 inches. He described the metal leaves carefully, these being placed next to each other "like bound pages of giant folios. Each leaf had writing on it, stamped and printed regularly as if by machine." [26]

According to Von Daniken all this was there for a purpose—"This metal library was created to outlast the ages, to remain legible for eternity." [27] He went on to suggest that the truths being brought to light might turn our dubious world picture completely upside down, and that *belief* in creation might be replaced by *knowledge* of creation—the history of man's origin might be entirely different from the "pious fairy story" which had been instilled into man. Von Daniken's imagination has gone wild.

Not only did Moricz claim that Von Daniken was lying, as he (Moricz) had never shown him those things, but he went on to say in regard to Von Daniken's assertions, "It was me who told him everything. He pumped me for hours on end." [28]

At the end of the *Encounter* article there is another penetrating observation: we learn that the legend of the "golden zoo" was actually known before Moricz talked about it to Von Daniken. It was first recounted thirty years ago "by a deranged army captain Jaramillo." [29]

## Von Daniken's Subjective Vision

It seems possible that Von Daniken was genuine at least in his subjective viewing of the golden animals and the metal plates. Although he did not see them literally, his fertile mind has the capacity to see things subjectively, then to propagate his views as though they should be as fully accepted by all who see only by normal vision. Von Daniken's imagination has really extended itself in his presentation, even in such "incidents" as having the guide order that all the flashlights be extinguished so they could be switched on once they actually entered the hall. This sort of embellishment added to the book's readability—so much the better, apparently! We stress that in the *Encounter* interview Moricz states clearly that they did not enter the cave— "It's blocked," Moricz told the interviewer. [30]

Von Daniken eventually admitted that he had not so much as been to the actual part of Ecuador he mentions, and had merely spent several hours below ground in a town that was 100 kilometers from the secret entrance through which he "journeyed" into the fabulous chamber with its golden zoo and fantastic library. "He further conceded that he could never have reached the said area by jeep in twenty-four hours, as he had recounted." [31]

However, Von Daniken insisted that all these things actually existed, and, as we have said, this has become his point of understanding the great "cosmic plan." He is the prophet to whom so much has been revealed, and his proclamations will stand despite the opposition of the scholars, whether they be archaeologists, theologians, or any others who are so foolish as to oppose that which the gods have made plain to a favorite son.

In *The Gold of the Gods* Von Daniken has at last found what he is looking for—the very message of the gods to men. The fact that his wild claims can easily be disproved does not seem to worry or embarrass him. He would not be the first to be ridiculed because of claims that were contrary to traditional beliefs, nor would he be the first to be rejected because he opposed the established order. After all, a successful man can laugh at his critics, laugh all the way to the bank.

Erich Von Daniken's chariots still crash: but somehow the shocks around the world have become less intense.

## CHAPTER 2

# The Mysterious Land of the Pharaohs

Although somewhat exaggerated, Erich Von Daniken gives an interesting statement about Egypt's origins:

> If we meekly accept the neat package of knowledge that the Egyptologists serve up to us, ancient Egypt appears suddenly and without transition with a fantastic ready-made civilization. Great cities and enormous temples, colossal statues with tremendous expressive power, splendid streets flanked by magnificent sculptures, perfect drainage systems, luxurious tombs carved out of the rock, pyramids of overwhelming size—these and many other wonderful things shot out of the ground, so to speak. Genuine miracles in a country that is suddenly capable of such achievements without recognizable prehistory! [1]

## The Mystery of Sudden Civilizations

The remarkable fact is that ancient civilizations do appear suddenly. The exception is the Hebrew people, for they know the origins of Abraham, their national father, and there are several chapters in the Bible outlining the major events of the earlier history relating to the area he came from, the area between the two rivers Euphrates and Tigris.

In those first chapters of Genesis the Hebrews trace their early beginnings to a man, Abraham, and beyond that to the mighty heroes of even earlier times. Other peoples trace their beginnings to dynasties and kingdoms already established, their earlier history lost in the mists of antiquity or folklore. Written records take us back only a little more than 5,000 years—beyond

3,000 B.C. such records are practically nonexistent.

Actually it may not be so very surprising that many civilizations appear suddenly. If there *was* a universal catastrophe such as the biblical flood, new civilizations would date from that time—or soon after. It is hard to find a better answer for so many civilizations coming to their first greatness at approximately the same general period of time.

Such a statement may at first seem totally unacceptable because of its religious overtones. However, the evidence is taken seriously by scholars. The record of that dispersion is in "the Table of Nations," at Genesis chapter 10, and one of the greatest archaeologists of all times, the late Professor W. F. Albright of Johns Hopkins University, had this to say about it:

> It stands absolutely alone in ancient literature without a remote parallel even among the Greeks . . . "The Table of Nations" remains an astonishingly accurate document . . . [It] shows such remarkably "modern" understanding of the ethnic and linguistic situation in the modern world, in spite of all its complexity, that scholars never fail to be impressed with the author's knowledge of the subject.[2]

Mizraim (Hebrew for "Egypt") is listed in that table as a son of Ham, who in turn was one of Noah's three sons. Because the Table of Nations is an important and accurate document relating to national beginnings, that early use of "Mizraim" in Genesis is an interesting clue.

It is all very intriguing, and we do not claim to have all the answers. Scholars have rethought many issues in the last twenty-five years. There are intertwining mysteries and problems associated with the known beginnings of early civilizations—even problems associated with the flora and fauna of different land masses are far from resolved.

## Writing on Clay and on Papyrus

Some of the cultural differences can be explained quite easily. A typical example is that of the different styles of writing between ancient Sumer and Egypt. In the land between the two rivers the whole culture was based on clay, and so writing developed by digging a stylus into the wet clay before it was baked. Thus wedge-shaped cuneiform letters developed, with an angular writing form that was quite different from the cursive style more commonly associated with Egypt.

Three basic scripts developed in Egypt. The first of these was hieroglyphics, which comes from two Greek words: *hieros* meaning "sacred," and *glyphein* meaning "to carve." Thus hieroglyphics were actually carvings or writings, especially by the priests. Sometimes they worked in stone, on the walls of temples and on various columns and monuments. At other times they painted directly on to stone, instead of carving.

Carving in stone was clumsy, and eventually Egypt gave to the world papyrus, reed paper. Strips of the papyrus reed were cut and woven, hammered out with a mallet, and left in the sun to dry. Then it was possible by using vegetable dyes to write across the face of this "paper," and so the Egyptians fostered this faster means of communication. A rapidly written cursive form known as hieratic was developed, with abbreviated characters and simpler forms. Comparison with hieroglyphics makes it clear that hieratic was a development of the older priestly form.

As time passed, hieratic gave over to a further abbreviated form, known as demotic, and this was used to a great extent for secular documents of various types. Hieroglyphics and demotic script were both used on the famous Rosetta Stone, found in 1799 by Napoleon's troops in the Egyptian town of Rosetta, on the western side of the Nile Delta. It was eventually deciphered by the Frenchman Jean François Champollion, in 1822.

Thus we see that it is possible to explain some of the cultural differences between these ancient civilizations on natural grounds—in Mesopotamia they pressed their styluses into clay, whereas in Egypt they used vegetable dyes and primitive "pens" to write across the face of the papyrus. The angular cuneiform developed in Sumerian clay, and the cursive hieratic and demotic found their way onto the papyrus sheets of Egypt.

This is given as an example, and also because it is an interesting fact of culture and development: often there were natural explanations for the way particular skills developed. Nevertheless, Erich Von Daniken's point as to the suddenness of the civilization in Egypt is basically correct. No matter which of the scholarly schools is right as to the exact dates of early dynasties, it is not challenged that the appearance of this magnificent Egyptian civilization was sudden.

One of the clearest evidences of the splendor of ancient Egypt is their whole series of pyramids. Over eighty are known up and down the Nile.

There are many pyramids around the world, but undoubtedly the best known are those of the Pharaohs of Egypt. Most scholars would date these to a period of some hundreds of years, commencing about 2700 B.C.

However, in modern times there has been considerable disagreement and debate as to the dates of Egyptian dynasties, and even as this new manuscript is being prepared, an interesting volume has come into the author's hands arguing for variations in some of the dates by about 400 years. One basic problem is that scholars are not agreed as to whether some dynasties followed each other, or were contemporary. According to this latter theory, at some periods of Egyptian history there were two rulers, each controlling different parts of the land at the same time. This would mean that the dynasty lists would have some sections parallel, rather than all sections being in strict chronological sequence.

## The Secrets of the Great Pyramid

Various writers have conjectured that the Great Pyramid was built by such biblical figures as Noah, Melchizedek, or Abraham. One argument is that Abraham went down to Egypt at the time of the great famine recorded in Genesis 12:10ff., and that the pyramid contained divine wisdom that was passed on to the Egyptians by a revelation of God through Abraham. Interesting as the theory may be, the timing is wrong. Abraham lived hundreds of years after the construction of the Great Pyramid.

In Roman times the writer Strabo referred to a secret entrance to this pyramid, and—partly based on this— in the Middle Ages a Muslim Caliph named Al-Ma'mun had his engineers blast their way into it. Though they did not find great treasures, they did demonstrate that inside there were long, secret passageways, and they actually found "the King's Chamber." However, no elaborate treasure was found, and one report was that the sarcophagus in which they would have expected to find the mummy of a Pharaoh was empty. Another report was that the Caliph found the mummy and tore it to pieces to recover the gold hidden with it. Yet another theory is that the pyramid had already been robbed, and that the mummy they found was not of Khufu who built the pyramid, but another Pharaoh who had been interred at a later time.

Through the ages, tomb robbers and others have searched for hidden treasures within this massive structure. As far as is known, no such treasures have been found, and even in the imposing "King's Chamber" with its empty stone sarcophagus there was no evidence of vandalism. If treasures were once buried with a Pharaoh in the Great Pyramid, their final fate is unknown.

*Napoleon and the Pyramids*

When Napoleon conquered Egypt, his engineers set out to make a map of the land, and they selected the Great Pyramid as a major point of triangulation. Among other interesting points, the engineers found that the east side of the pyramid pointed due east, and was directly aligned to the polar axis of the earth.

Undoubtedly this pyramid was the most magnificent of all those constructed. Its sides were almost a perfect square, and Napoleon's engineers were right—the pyramid's sides were within one tenth of a degree of being set toward true north-south and east-west.

It is usually conjectured that the builders found true north by utilizing an artificial horizon.[3] A circular wall would be built, it being high enough for a person sitting inside not to be able to see anything on the ground on the other side of the wall.

This seated person would have his head behind the center of the wall. He would watch until a bright northerly star rose, and would direct another observer to mark the place of its appearance on the wall. He would continue to watch, and when the star set, another mark would be made. Then a plumb bob would be lowered from each of those two marks, so that the two points on the floor, immediately below those marks, could be fixed. From these the surveyors would draw lines to the center of the circular wall. Next they would bisect the angle between those two lines, and thus ascertain true north.

It is interesting to put this alongside a quotation from Charles Berlitz:

> An unusual indication of the age of the pyramid exists in its orientation to the North Star, clearly visible up through the millions of tons of perfectly set rock through the Grand Gallery which goes up to an opening at the upper side of the pyramid directly from the King's Chamber. Evi-

dence has been offered that the North Star at the
time it was "captured" in the pyramid's sights was
in the Dragon Constellation and has since become
part of the Big Dipper, itself a part of the Great
Bear.[4]

In the same context Berlitz suggests that apparently
the Great Pyramid was "a tremendous seasonal clock
and calendar." He shows how the varying lengths of the
shadows resulting from the pyramid's slightly concave
shape indicated "the arrival of the spring equinox, the
passing of the year, and even the hours of the day." [5]

These great mysteries of the past are often associated
with the seasons. Much of the worship of peoples of old
centered around the sun, the moon, and the stars. It
was recognized that the seasonal movements of the
heavenly bodies were very relevant for farming and
other such activities.

## The Development of Pyramidology

Since the Napoleonic reports referred to above, a cult
of pyramidology has developed. The Great Pyramid
has been painstakingly measured by archaeologists, surveyors, astronomers, engineers, cartographers, and
various others who have offered their "special" interpretations of the pyramid's statistics. Fortunes have
been spent to give out some of these "secrets."

One of the best known proponents of pyramidology
was Colonel Howard Voise, who in the 1830s used
gunpowder to blast his way into the Great Pyramid.
From his measurements the theory was evolved that
this pyramid had actually been built by Noah and his
sons under divine guidance, and that it incorporated
cosmic wisdom. The publisher John Taylor wrote at
length about these theories, and convinced the Scottish
astronomer Charles Piazzi Smyth of the religious value
of these measurements and interpretations.

Smyth went to Egypt to confirm the theories he was

now espousing, and spent several months, with instruments made especially for the project, measuring the pyramid and its environs. He claimed that the sides were perfect equilateral triangles, and he gave out a number of fascinating figures, such as there being 36,524 "pyramid inches" around the square at the base. He pointed out that this was almost exactly one hundred times the number of days there are in a year—an interesting surmise only so long as we accept his fundamental assumption of a "pyramid inch." He made much of other statistics, such as the height of the pyramid being 1/270,000 of the earth's circumference, which in turn was supposedly one-billionth of the distance from the earth to the sun.

He and his colleagues also insisted that the empty stone sarcophagus originally found in the King's Chamber was actually a standard of measurement, a system they worked out by a remarkably complex series of calculations.

However, the theories are not very convincing, for the whole idea of a pyramid inch is Smyth's own invention. Even if we were to accept these remarkable figures as to the relationship between the pyramid's measurements and the distance to the sun, we would have to ignore the more recent measurements which indicate that although Smyth did a fine job with the instruments available to him, his figures certainly would not be considered very accurate in our computer age. His measurements have been revised considerably.

Smyth claimed that a system of measurements involving the empty sarcophagus was actually the ancestor to the British system of volume, but this is incapable of belief. That sarcophagus would have held something like one and a quarter tons of water: to base a theory about standards of measurement on an ancient coffin that had been shut up inside an artificial mountain for centuries is ludicrous.

*The Prophets Who Failed*

Smyth's measurements were carried over into religious realms, and were even related to Christian teachings. He calculated from his measurements that a great miracle was to take place in 1881—possibly the second coming of Christ or the establishment of His millennial kingdom. However, 1881 came and went, and the miracle did not occur.

In his early manhood the great Egyptologist W. M. Flinders Petrie was somewhat taken in by Smyth's theories, because his father had adopted them. However, Petrie undertook his own investigations. He went to Egypt and showed that Smyth's measurements were seriously inaccurate, despite the expensive instruments that had been constructed especially for the project. This meant that the whole basis was disproved, but the theories persisted. Flinders Petrie reported that one cultist even attempted to reduce the size of a granite figure located in the vestibule of the burial chamber— its size opposed his theories!

Despite Petrie's demonstration that Smyth's figures were unacceptable, pyramidology did not die. A new leader named David Davidson soon used Petrie's figures instead of Smyth's, and, with certain other figures in the King List of the ancient Egyptian historian Manetho, was able to propagate new prophetic teachings. A great world war was supposed to break out in 1928, and Christ would return to the earth in 1936. Although these years also passed without the prophecies being fulfilled, cultists do not give up easily, and again the numbers were adjusted. A new prediction was given out that the world would come to an end in 1953.

Von Daniken also joins the ranks of those who discuss the remarkable facts that can be deduced from the measurements of the Great Pyramid, and then he caustically suggests, "The unparalleled 'classical' dimensions of the pyramid occurred to the master builder by chance." [6]

However, Sprague and Catherine de Camp state:

It has often been shown that with enough figures to juggle, one can readily extract cosmic results from unlikely material. Borchardt, as an anti-Pyramidological joke, derived the base e of natural logarithms from the slope of Sahura's pyramid. Barnard, by juggling the dimensions of the Temple of Artemis at Ephesus, got the moon's diameter, the length of the lunar month, and the date of the building.[7]

It is almost pathetic to put another Von Daniken argument alongside the above quotation. He asks:

Yet who is so ingenuous as to believe that the pyramid was nothing but the tomb of a king? From now on, who will consider the transmission of mathematical and astronomical signs as pure chance? [8]

Smyth's hypothetical "pyramid inch," the system of measurements based on an empty sarcophagus, the often-changing prophecies based on those "astronomical signs" in the Great Pyramid, are sufficient indications that Von Daniken's questions need not be taken seriously.

## How the Pyramid Building Style Developed

Let it be clearly stated that we accept without reservation that the Great Pyramid was a remarkable construction. Its builders did not have modern powerful machinery or concrete and structural steel: they were restricted to such instruments as copper saws and chisels, and did not have modern surveying equipment. However, the capacity of men of old is not radically different from that of modern men, and occasionally there arises a genius whose memory lives on. One such was Imhotep, who is credited with the construction of the famous Step Pyramid at Saqqara for Pharaoh Zozer. Imhotep was a genius, famous as a statesman, physician, and builder. He was later deified as the God of Medicine.

Before the time of Imhotep and Zozer, the kings and nobles of Egypt were buried in mastabas—brick structures, rectangular in shape, having walls that sloped inward; they were built over the underground chamber where the king would be buried. The first real pyramid, the Step Pyramid at Saqqara, began as a mastaba but was twice enlarged so that it eventually took the form of several different mastabas on top of each other, so becoming the Step Pyramid. Eventually it had six stages and was some 200 feet high, with a base approximately twice that size.

Other Pharaohs followed Zozer's elaborate example, and a series of pyramids came into being. These massive constructions were normally built with four sides forming a rectangular base, the sides rising until they met at a point that theoretically was over the center of the structure at ground level.

The most famous of the Egyptian pyramids are the three large ones at Gizeh, outside Cairo. These three pyramids are traditionally believed to have been constructed as the burial places for Pharaohs Khufu, Khafre, and Menkaure. There are several smaller pyramids in the same general area.

The largest of this group of pyramids was that of Pharaoh Khufu, known as Cheops in Greek writings. This "Great Pyramid" is a remarkable edifice, one of the seven wonders of the world and the best preserved of the seven. It was Khufu's masterpiece, called Khuit-Khufu, literally meaning "Khufu's horizon." The ancient historians Herodotus and Manetho tell us that Khufu was the builder, and in addition his name is painted on some of its inside stones.

Like Zozer before him, Khufu changed his mind at

various points while the pyramid was being constructed. The usual underground chamber associated with the earlier mastabas was apparently abandoned after having been dug out of the solid rock. Another room was then added—it is still pointed out as "the Queen's Chamber," though probably this identification is not correct. This chamber also was not completed, and a third room was added, now known as "the King's Chamber." This was higher up in the pyramid. Various theories have been put forward to explain why these changes were made, one being that the Pharaoh was a claustrophobe and wanted to lie nearer the sun, rather than being buried deep underground as had been done with earlier Pharaohs.

The King's Chamber is eighteen feet high and measures sixteen feet by thirty-three and one half feet. The roof is formed by nine granite slabs that weigh about thirty tons each.

Erich Von Daniken implies that it is ingenuous "to believe that the pyramid was nothing but the tomb of a king." [9] However, the very fact that an empty sarcophagus was found indicates that one purpose of the pyramid was that it would be such a tomb. Certain it is that the pyramids in general were tombs for Pharaohs and royal personages. There were about eighty-five different pyramids, and approximately forty-five mummified bodies have been recovered. The pyramids were apparently meant as great memorials to the rulers who were interred in these huge masses of stone.

## Building the Great Pyramid

How were these massive memorials actually constructed? We shall concern ourselves especially with the Great Pyramid, supposedly constructed by Khufu (Cheops) as a sepulcher for himself and his queen. Traditionally it is believed that he both planned and commenced its erection as soon as he succeeded to the throne.

It has been estimated that there were about two and a half million blocks used in the construction of this Great Pyramid. The blocks were marked with the location where they were to be placed in the pyramid itself, and they were cut so precisely that when many of the stones were fitted, the joints were barely perceptible.

However, accounts of how closely the stones fitted are at times exaggerated. The core stones were only roughly fitted together, and the joints between the blocks were often quite pronounced. It seems that the rows of huge stones were first lined up next to each other on the ground, then trimmed to fit before they were hauled into place. It was the outside blocks of limestone casing that were fitted together so accurately that the blade of a knife could hardly be fitted between them. As the earth of the ramp was eventually pulled away, no doubt the stonemasons would clear off any other irregularities that had been left in the limestone facings covering the entire outside of the pyramid. Much of this limestone has been removed in past ages, for building houses and other constructions.

The huge amount of limestone required would have come from Troyu across the Nile, whereas the granite had to be brought down from the area we now know as Aswan. It was rafted down the Nile, then hauled on wooden sleds to the site of the pyramid itself.

Von Daniken also stated that it would have been more practical for the pyramids to be built nearer the eastern quarries so that the transport distances would be shortened. However, this overlooks the reason for selecting the west bank of the Nile for the location of the pyramids—ancient Egyptians looked toward the setting sun in the west as the dwelling place of the dead.

The technology of these people was remarkable, for we know that even at the time of the First Dynasty, probably about 3100 B.C., they used copper saws that cut through limestone. Most of the massive stones in the pyramids are limestone, and it was relatively easily obtained from stone quarries on the Nile, the smaller stones weighing about two tons but some being as heavy as twelve tons.

## The Questions of Erich Von Daniken

At this point we pause to consider some of Erich Von Daniken's questions about the construction of the Great Pyramid. He tells us that blocks weighing twelve tons could not be pushed up a ramp with nonexistent ropes on nonexistent rollers, with a host of workers who lived on nonexistent grain and slept in nonexistent huts. Nor could they complete their work by the "heave-ho" method, utilizing a nonexistent loudspeaker. He suggests that if this method had been utilized this pyramid would have taken 664 years to complete.[10]

He tells us that stone blocks used in the building of the Great Pyramid could not have been moved on wooden rollers because "the Egyptians could scarcely have felled and turned into rollers the few trees, mainly palms that then (as now) grew in Egypt, because the dates from the palms were urgently needed for food and the trunks and fronds were the only things giving shade to the dried-up ground." [11] He suggests that enormous difficulties were involved in the importing of wood.

As for this argument (that the Egyptians did not import timber), in his widely read *Ancient Near Eastern Texts,* Professor J. Pritchard shows that Senefru, the father of Cheops, sent some forty ships to Phoenicia for the express purpose of importing coniferous timber.[12]

Not only do we know that wood was imported, but we also know that wooden sleds were utilized in ancient Egypt: so also was wooden scaffolding. In his important book, *The Pyramids of Egypt,* I. E. S. Edwards tells of wooden balks being found *in situ* at Lisht. The point is, wood was used extensively in ancient Egypt.

Erich Von Daniken claims that the twelve-ton stones in the Great Pyramid could not have been moved without modern lifting machinery (unless astronaut help was available!). The average size of the stones in the pyramid was two and one half tons, but, as we saw above, some were as heavy as twelve tons. However, there are many known examples from other countries where heavier stones have been lifted by quite simple means, with a small number of workmen.

## Moving a Sixty-Ton Statue

In Egypt itself there is an especially interesting picture from the Tomb of Djehutihotep, a nobleman who lived in the time of the Twelfth Dynasty of Egypt. It is of a huge statue of Djehutihotep himself, estimated to have weighed about sixty tons. It is mounted on a wooden sled, and is being pulled by 172 men. Water or some other liquid is being poured on the ground, apparently to lessen the friction and to make the haulage easier. If a sixty-ton statue could be moved with a relatively small number of men, it stands to reason that the two and a half-ton stones for the Great Pyramid could have been moved much more easily.

Another point that Von Daniken made is that it would take 664 years to build the Great Pyramid, but this is nonsense. Some of the smaller pyramids have names of Pharaohs and dates on them. The Pyramid of Meidum has different dates at various points of its construction, and another pyramid at Dahshur has a foundation date inscribed on it. This states it was laid in the twenty-first year of Pharaoh Senefru, and about halfway up there is a second date which is in the same Pharaoh's twenty-second year.

Clearly nothing like 664 years is necessary for the building of the Great Pyramid, as Von Daniken suggests. The ancient historian Herodotus said that it took ten years to build the causeway from the Nile to the pyramid, and then another twenty years to build the pyramid itself. By the time of Herodotus the pyramids were long since ancient, and some of the tales he was told as a tourist were clearly not to be taken seriously. This account of ten years plus twenty years, with 100,000 workmen, was possibly in that category. Modern calculations suggest that the Great Pyramid could have been built in less than ten years. As a matter of interest, Cheops's reign extended over twenty-three years.

One of the well-known theories as to how the blocks were put into position was that pulleys and ropes were utilized, together with embankments of earth. Men standing on a prepared flat surface at the top would drag the blocks up from the desert floor. As the height of the pyramid was increased, so the earth ramp would also be increased against the stones recently laid. The earth was removed when the pyramid was completed.

Many of the claims made about the Great Pyramid are extreme. We have shown above that Pyramidology cannot always be taken as seriously as some of its proponents would desire—we have already referred to Von Daniken's espousal of some aspects of this subject.

## The Heave-Ho Method

As for his argument that the pyramid stones could not have been moved by the so-called heave-ho method, I personally have watched huge stones being moved from recent excavations at Karnak, farther up the Nile than most of the pyramids. The foreman chanted a few numbers and then gave the order to heave. One single rope and a simple pulley was used, with about ten men pulling and pushing on a very large stone. This method is being utilized in modern times, and there is no reason why it would not have worked in the days when the pyramids were being built.

Von Daniken referred to the workmen using "non-existent rope," but rope was known in Egypt before the time of Pharaoh Zozer's Step Pyramid, and it is usually accepted that this pyramid predated the Great Pyramid by about seventy years.

Ropes, pulleys, wooden sleds, sufficient workmen, reasonable accommodation, extra labor at certain seasons when "welfare work" was undertaken (while the Nile was in flood), Egyptian troops, dates on tombs, mummies in many of the pyramids—it all adds up to convincing evidence that these pyramids were the remarkable achievements of men who lived long ago: there is no evidence of help from astronauts or visitors from other planets. Nor did such astronauts leave behind any of their new metals.

## Embalming and the Gods

Almost before Von Daniken has raised his own ponderous questions about the construction of the pyramids, he moves on to the subject of embalming. He tells us: "Mummies, equally incomprehensible and not yet convincingly explained, stare at us from the remote past as if they held some magic secret." [13]

Von Daniken has the answer—"the 'gods' promised to return from the stars in order to awaken the well-preserved bodies to new life. That is why the provisioning of the embalmed corpses in the burial chambers took such a practical form, and was intended for a life on this side of the grave." [14] As he goes on, Von Daniken reproduces for us the possible thoughts of a Pharaoh who knew about the gods and resolved to make for himself a burial place that would not be destroyed for thousands of years: it would also be visible far across the country. The Pharaoh is supposed to think to himself: "The gods promised to return and wake me up (or doctors in the distant future will discover a way to restore me to life again)." [15]

Von Daniken then goes on to talk about dogs being deep-frozen for a week, being thawed out, and living on "as cheerfully as ever." [16]

We are then reminded of the modern ideas of bodies being deep-frozen until science can remove the cause of death and restore the bodies to new life. Von Daniken asks, "Or did some 'gods' (space travelers) transmit to a quick-witted prince of royal blood their knowledge of how corpses can be reawakened after a special treatment?" [17]

So the whole idea caught on and "in the course of the centuries, mummification, originally a solemn matter, became the fashion. Suddenly everyone wanted to be reawakened; suddenly everyone thought that he would come to new life so long as he did the same as his forefathers. The high priests, who actually did possess some knowledge of such reawakenings, did a great deal to encourage this cult, for their class did good business out of it." [18]

Von Daniken's hypothesis is nonsensical—unless we can think of a body preserved without a brain or internal organs. Anyone who has seen the mummies in the Cairo Museum—as I have done—must agree at this point. Ancient Pharaohs such as Ramses the Great and Seti I lie in the Mummy Room, looking for all the world like ghastly pieces of leather over the top of wizened human features. They were preserved as well as human skill allowed, but it did not prevent the decay of their very mortal frames.

The practice of embalming was designed to arrest the decomposition of the body so that it could enjoy life after death and utilize the various objects buried with it in the tomb. Although the process of mummification has varied in some of its details over the centuries, it usually involved the removal of most of the internal organs. These were put into funerary jars, the corpse itself being saturated in a carefully prepared solution for a number of weeks. The body was packed with various preservatives, and was plastered over with something similar to our modern plaster of Paris before it was wrapped in the familiar mummy bindings.

This practice developed from the observation of the bodies of dead animals being preserved in the dry sands of Egypt. Man hoped to live on beyond death, and clumsily he did his best to preserve the human body. To attribute such primitive efforts to visiting deities is ludicrous—unless the Egyptians were extremely gullible.

## The Chariots Still Crash

The pyramid age passed, and some of the greatest Pharaohs were not buried in pyramids—a good example being Rameses II who was buried in the Valley of the Kings. Probably the Pharaohs turned away from the idea of pyramids because such sites were too inviting to future tomb robbers.

In this connection Charles Berlitz states:

> In general, pyramids are considered, along with obelisks, to be related to sun worship, by marking the sun's progress in the day and year. "Sun boats" for the buried Pharaohs to follow the sun into heaven have been found buried near some of the pyramids, exactly pointed on a west-east axis.[19]

So much for Erich Von Daniken's *Chariots of the Gods?,* those heavenly vehicles in which the Pharaohs were to take their continuing journey. In this case the chariots turn out to be nothing more than sun boats and the Pharaohs themselves had already ordered their construction. This was their feeble preparation for the time when they, the supposed earthly representatives of the sun god Ra, would rejoin him in the land beyond the pyramids.

The chariots of the Pharaohs were land-based after all. And Erich Von Daniken's chariots still crash, this time into the pyramids of ancient Egypt.

## CHAPTER 3

# Easter Island Tells Its Tale

Who made those huge statues on Easter Island? How were they carved out of the living rock? Who moved them several miles across the plain so that they could be placed on the cliff's face, looking out across the ocean?

## Weird Statues on a Lonely Outcropping

These are only some of the questions that could be asked about Easter Island and its gigantic statues. For years they have been fruitful ground for mystic groups and occult societies, and have been the subject of a number of films and books. As long ago as 1898, Frederick Spencer Oliver published an occult novel entitled *A Dweller on Two Planets,* and it led to rumors of a supposed people from the lost land of Lemuria performing their mystic rites in northern California. The relevance of this (and of similar writings) to Easter Island is that those weird statues on a lonely outcropping of land in the South Pacific have been put forward by occultists as irrefutable evidence that there was such a lost land.

Undoubtedly there have been mysteries about Easter Island, and not all of them have been resolved. The island itself is over 2,000 miles from the South American coast, and in the other direction to the west it is 1,200 miles to Pitcairn Island. Its total area is forty-five square miles: it is about fifteen miles across, and thirty-five miles in circumference. It has three extinct volcanoes, known as Rano Raraku, Rano Kao, and Rano Arori, and a freshwater lake is in the crater of each of them.

The name Easter Island stems from the fact that a Dutch admiral, Jakob Roggeven, landed there on Easter Sunday in 1722. The local people call it Rapa Nui, a name given by the first Tahitians who landed there in the 1870s. They gave it this name (which means "Great Rapa") because they thought it looked like the smaller Rapa Iti in the Tubai Islands. The island is volcanic, with its soil consisting of decomposed lava.

Easter Island's famous statues with huge heads range from about three to thirty-six feet in height. Even though many of them have been removed for display in far-away museums, there are still over 600 on the island. Many of the larger ones are unfinished, and hundreds of chisels and other stone tools for shaping them lie around in the quarries.

## A Lost Continent? Land Bridges over the Ocean?

Another popular writer was James Churchward, especially with his *Lost Continent of Mu,* published in 1926. He claimed that a Hindu priest had translated the mysterious Naacal Tablets for him, though in his writings he alternates between India and Tibet as to where he actually "saw" the tablets. He improved on the sunken continent hypothesis of earlier writers, and now offered his readers two such continents—Atlantis which was somewhere in the Atlantic, and Mu in the Pacific, this latter being the Lemuria of occult writers. He claimed that Easter Island was actually a south-eastern extension of this lost continent.

It is interesting to notice that in 1923 it was reported that Easter Island had disappeared beneath the sea, but eventually the report was proved wrong. A ship's navigator had simply been off course!

Other writers conjectured that there had been land bridges, each extending for a thousand miles, built by the advanced Lemurians who lived on the continent that was now submerged. However, archaeologists and oceanographers are emphatic that there is no possibility of a submerged continent in either the Eastern or Central Pacific, for this ocean is very deep except where volcanic islands have been forced up to the surface. Continental-type rocks are not found in the Pacific, and theories as to magnificent causeways and sunken continents have been disproved.

## Early Writing Found on Easter Island

That is not to say that the knowledge and expertise of these Pacific Islanders was not remarkable—it was indeed. Apart altogether from their famous statues, they had a system of writing that involved over 500 signs, and some scholars believe that the origin of this writing is as great a mystery as that of the island's better-known statues. It has been claimed that their writing not only had similarities to that used in the Caroline Islands, but also to the script of the Indus Valley, halfway around the world.

The Indus Valley region is the general area of Mohenjo-Daro and Harappa, civilizations extending back into the third millennia B.C., and including well-planned cities that even had a system for the disposal of waste. In discussing this, Charles Berlitz comments:

The Indus Valley culture is thought to be contemporaneous with ancient Sumeria, the script of which we can read, but the writing of Mohenjo-Daro and Harappa has proved indecipherable, since the language itself has disappeared, along with the people who spoke it.[1]

Berlitz reminds us that when Easter Island was first visited in modern times some of the islanders could still read this mysterious writing, but now all who could read it have died and the secret of the writing has died with them. Berlitz presents over twenty symbols which are virtually the same in both the Easter Island and the ancient Indus Valley scripts.

This suggestion that the written script of the Easter Islanders has similarities to that of the ancient Sumerians is very interesting. A possible explanation is tied to the biblical story of the Tower of Babel and the confusion of man's language, for archaeology confirms the general pattern of the influence and culture of the ancient Mesopotamian people spreading far and wide as men scattered over the face of the earth. Some of the languages known in the Ancient Near East and elsewhere appear to have first developed in the land between the two rivers.

## *The Tower of Babel, Languages, and Easter Island*

Professor W. F. Albright suggested that the story of the Tower of Babel should be dated to the twenty-second century B.C., and in a discussion of some of the terminology in the Bible record he concluded, "It was, therefore, as a tremendous monument to its builders that the Tower of Babel was intended." [2] He took the record seriously.

There are a number of traditions around the world as to the Tower of Babel and the confusion of man's language. Robert T. Boyd quotes a tablet referring to King Ur-Nammu of the Third Dynasty of Ur, supposedly receiving orders from his god to build a great temple tower.[3] The conjectured date is in the twenty-first century B.C. Boyd goes on to refer to a tablet telling of the displeasure of the gods: they destroyed the great tower, scattered men abroad, and confused their language.

As seen above, Professor Albright suggested the twenty-second century B.C. for the Babel incident, and the Ur date quoted by Robert Boyd is remarkably close. Dating that extends back into the third millennia B.C. is not yet exact, and this is an interesting approximation. Traditions such as this about man's dispersal have bases in fact, and a surprising number of "new" civilizations that suddenly appear are dated to approximately 2000 B.C. It may be more than coincidence.

It is a fact that there has been a great change in scholarly thinking about some sudden happening, and a consequent dispersion of culture and of language. Could this incident explain the mysterious relationship between the script of Easter Island and that of the Indus Valley civilization? At first sight this seems entirely out of the question, for the dates do not agree. However, that also is something of an open question.

Three levels of culture have been identified at Easter Island, and no one really knows the date of the earliest settlement there—which, incidentally, was more remarkably developed than its two later successors. The Carbon-14 tests on Thor Heyerdahl's materials related to a later level, and though scholarly proposals for the earliest level tend to settle for a date nearer to our time than the early Indus Valley civilizations, we do not really know.

As Charles Berlitz says, "The existence of a script isolated on an island thousands of miles from any land in the world's largest ocean, halfway around the world from a similar script of prehistoric West India, implies not only a common origin, but a diffusion of culture, and is a fairly concrete indication of unrecorded early sea voyages of a range and scope previously considered impossible." [4]

## An Ancient Ship

The incident of the Tower of Babel would not necessarily preclude normal transport, and possibly the original voyage to Easter Island was by ship (and not in a chariot of the gods!). Bible miracles do not necessarily involve only supernatural powers. Forces of nature, combinations of circumstances, human compulsions— these and other factors can harmonize so that there is a perfect synchronization and the Divine will is accomplished. This is not to limit the reality of miracles for which there is no normal explanation. If one can believe in God, it is logical that he also believes in the possibility of Divine miracles in the fullest sense. We do not always know the means by which the miracle is brought to us.

On one of the early stone carvings at Easter Island an ancient ship can clearly be seen, complete with three masts. It is a much larger type of ship than those used by the natives of the island when it was first visited in modern times. Thor Heyerdahl has a colored picture of this carving in his popular book *Aku-Aku*. Perhaps that ship is a clue to the means by which Easter Island was first settled as men obeyed a strange compulsion they could not resist.

The suggestion that ancient people settled on Easter Island as long ago as Sumerian times will not meet with immediate agreement among scholars. Indeed, most would suggest that Easter Island has been inhabited for only a few hundred years, though others will allow a longer period. Sprague and Catherine de Camp argue as follows:

> Sober scientists have also searched for the truth about the settlement of Easter Island. They are now convinced that the Polynesians anciently lived along the southeast coasts of Asia—in South China, Indo-China, or Malaya. The rise of a powerful Chinese Empire in the second millennium B.C. touched off a general movement of peoples. Each tribe on the fringes of Chinese civilization, fleeing from advancing Chinese imperialism, crowded its neighbors outward. Because the Polynesians were already spread along the coast, they could go nowhere but across the sea. Probably their flight was speeded by the fact that they were still in the Stone Age when their enemies, the Mongoloid peoples, had metal weapons.[5]

## How Explain Racial Mixtures?

We read on and find that the Polynesians are a relatively uniform race, combining Caucasoid, Mongoloid, and Negroid traits. Where did such a combining of racial types originate? Traditionally the link is to the three sons of Noah—Shem (Caucasoid), Ham (Negroid), and Japheth (Mongoloid). Our knowledge about these early Easter Island people is relatively limited, and insistence on very late dates really depends on Carbon-14 and similar dating systems. In our next chapter we shall see that these are often highly suspect.

Relatively soon after the Flood, the Bible says that men were dispersed far and wide. Their languages were confused at the time of the building of the Tower of Babel. It is by no means impossible that this is when Polynesian peoples first settled in the islands of the Pacific, and when Australian aborigines first arrived in the great island continent "Down Under."

Another point should be mentioned. In the above quotation from Robert T. Boyd's book, the incident of the Tower of Babel is associated with the worship of the moon god Nannar. Astronomical patterns have been pointed out with the statues of Easter Island, the remarkably long lines across the Plain of Nazca, the huge monoliths at Stonehenge in England, the ziggurat (temple tower) at Ur and other cities in ancient Mesopotamia—and at various sites in Latin America: there are such associations in many ancient civilizations around the world.

If that story of Babel happened to be true, would men have stopped building their temples into the sky? Of course not. Many of them would start again, using the knowledge and experience of their previous culture. They would continue their worship of the sun, the moon, and the stars as in their early home of Sumer. To say the least, the great similarities in buildings and in languages among many of the peoples around the world are remarkable.

## The Possibility of a Parent Language

Charles Berlitz has an interesting comment about man's common language heritage:

> Almost all the languages of Europe and some of those of the Middle East as far as India are connected, both through vocabulary and construction; they probably are descended from a parent language beyond history which has given common features to them all. . . . The recurrent legend of the Tower of Babel on both sides of the ocean may be a common memory of the disappearance of an older language . . .[6]

Berlitz goes on to quote from various ancient records to show amazing similarities that can hardly be accounted for by chance contact. As he elaborates this subject, statements such as the following become almost commonplace:

> Even more striking are the word similarities between Hawaiian and ancient Greek which appear to indicate that seafarers, speaking ancient Greek or a similar language, sailed an ocean that, as far as we know, the Greeks of history did not even know existed.[7]

Those "word similarities" have surprised linguists and translators over and over again. The coincidences and similarities are beyond explanation by the glib use of terms such as "imitation," and "borrowing." Both of these concepts are part of the answer, but they are insufficient of themselves to explain the worldwide phenomena. What links were there with that early civilization before men were scattered across the globe?

## The Ten Kings before the Flood

Another relevant comment from Berlitz is as follows:

When the first Spanish navigators reached the Canary Islands in the fourteenth century they found remnants of an advanced, well-organized Stone Age culture, including such "Atlantean" elements as stone buildings, a written script, sun worship, mummies, bull fights and even ten elected kings, reminiscent of the Ten Kings of Atlantis mentioned by Plato and the Ten Kings of the Maya.[8]

Thinking again of that incident of the Tower of Babel, it could also be added that these "ten kings" referred to in the above quotation might well be reminiscent of the ten kings of the "Kish King List" of ancient Sumeria—a list that referred to "the ten kings who lived before the Flood." The reference to the Ten Kings of the Maya could indicate that the earliest Mayan culture should also be dated back to those times referred to in the Bible.

At Genesis chapter 5, there is another remarkable point of similarity. Ten successive "fathers" are listed— Adam is the first, and Noah is the tenth. Then came the Flood. What are we to make of these recurring statements about ten kings (or fathers) who lived before the Flood? How are we to explain cultural links between Sumer, the Indus Valley civilizations, Easter Island, the Mayas, and so many others?

Did some of their forefathers take part in the building of a huge structure that was to reach into the very heights of heaven? In that incident of the Tower of Babel have we a clue as to when many of the first settlers arrived in their way-off homes across the sea? Did they follow some strange compulsion so that they adopted new surroundings, with an expanse of ocean where before their vision had been limited to the baked clay of the land between the two rivers?

The resemblances are not limited to language or buildings, as can be shown from many of the ancient records. Harold Gladwyn in his book *Men Out of Asia* outlines some of the musical elements common in the old world and the new. A musical instrument made of reeds in ancient Greece is virtually the same as one played today in the Solomon Islands of the Pacific, and also in the highlands of the Andes. He tells us that not only is there an almost identical structure, but even the pitch is the same in these instruments that are spread so far across the world.

## Easter Islanders not Peruvians

If we completely discount the Tower of Babel as explaining the origin of the Easter Islanders, where *did* they come from? It is relevant to state that it is unlikely that the Polynesians on Easter Island were the descendants of Peruvian Indians. Peruvians are essentially a short people, with copper-colored skins and straight hair, whereas the Polynesians are basically tall, brown-skinned, with wavy hair and very muscular bodies. In any case, Peruvians made little use of the sea, partly because the west coast of South America does not have many good harbors, and it is renowned for its treacherous surf. It is possible that they sailed across the Pacific on balsa rafts, but, despite Thor Heyerdahl's successful voyage, it is by no means certain that this is the explanation for the arrival of the first settlers on Easter Island.

A great deal of public interest was aroused by that famous voyage of Thor Heyerdahl's in 1947, when he and five Scandinavian friends sailed from Peru on a raft of balsa logs. They voyaged over 4,000 miles across the Pacific until they reached the Tuamotu Archipelago. Heyerdahl believed that his Nordic ancestors had moved out from northern Europe, settled in Peru, founded the original civilization of the Andes, and eventually set out on rafts across the Pacific until they found and settled the Polynesian Islands. Part of his theory was based on ancient traditions about tall, blond, pale-skinned and blue-eyed peoples who had visited these various "new" civilizations in ancient times.

Such legends are common with many peoples, and, although it is interesting, many scholars doubt the basic validity of the theory. One opposing argument—not entirely convincing as to some of the legends—relates to the importance placed on a fair skin. Through the centuries, dark skins have been associated with work out in the sun, and therefore with the laboring classes. A person with a fair skin was supposedly a superior being, such as one of the aristocracy, and there are even known cases of girls being imprisoned in huts so that their skins would be bleached white.

Though Thor Heyerdahl's theory about Nordic people moving out from Peru is not accepted in all scholarly circles, he has made an outstanding contribution to knowledge by his study of the Easter Island statues.

Some of the 600 statues still lying around Easter Island would weigh as much as fifty tons, and even the "hats" weigh several tons.

## Astronaut Help not Needed

Various arguments have been put forward to suggest that the Easter Islanders could not have built their famous statues without outside help. Erich Von Daniken declared that the island could not have supported more than 2,000 people. Thor Heyerdahl suggests that it could have supported 7,000, but, even if the smaller figure were accepted, Heyerdahl's accomplishments showed that the statues could still be built by the local people without modern methods or Von Daniken's "astronaut" help.

In his book *Aku-Aku* Thor Heyerdahl gives the answers to a number of problems, and even includes relevant colored photographs to prove some of his points.

The local people believed that the statues were originally made by the early settlers known as "the Long Ears," and the mayor of Easter Island was descended from this group. On the promise of one hundred dollars, he and several relatives underwent religious rituals as preparation for the work they agreed to do. Then they attacked the volcanic stone with the flint axes that were there in abundance, flaking off the rock as the outline of a new statue was formed.

Heyerdahl states that by the third day the contours of the new statue were "clearly visible on the rock wall." The mayor estimated that it would have taken a year to complete one statue, using six men. Heyerdahl's group was able to be there for only a much shorter period, and so the statue was not completed. However, the technique had been effectively demonstrated.

Heyerdahl also showed how these huge statues could be stood on end, not needing thousands of helpers or modern lifting equipment as Von Daniken had claimed was necessary if astronaut help was not available. The mayor with eleven men showed how this could be done. Three large wooden poles were used at first, then only two. One of the medium-sized statues, selected from the hundreds lying on the ground, was lifted a fraction of an inch by the helpers, while the mayor himself forced a few small stones beneath it. This process was continually repeated over several days, with the stones getting larger and larger and the statue itself roped into place so that it would not topple over. After eighteen days the process had been completed, and the giant statue rested quietly in its upright position.

## *About Putting on Hats . . . and*
## *"An Empty Soap Box"*

Another problem discussed through the years relates to the large stone caps that are fitted on top of the

statues. Some writers have suggested they are not caps,
but that, as they are red in color, they represent the
red hair of the "models"—possibly the forebears of the
builders.

Erich Von Daniken made much of the problem of
how these "caps" could be deposited on top of the
statues, but this also was answered by Thor Heyerdahl.
At various points on the island he found earth ramps
*in situ*—and some of the stone caps were also still
there, discarded. After the statue itself had been erected
by the original workers, a ramp was built against it.
Then the cap was hauled up backward, and finally it
was toppled over so that it would sit directly on the
head of the statue.

Heyerdahl had shown that the statues could be made
by a few men, and could even be maneuvered into an
upright position by a small group. However, Von
Daniken also argued that it was beyond the strength of
a relatively few men to haul such a statue seven miles
across the plain to the cliff's edge, where so many of
the statues are situated today.

As with the other points, Thor Heyerdahl had given
the answer to this problem before Von Daniken's first
book became widely known. Heyerdahl organized a
great feast for many of the villagers, and afterward 180
men took their places on a long rope that had been
attached to the neck of the selected statue. There were
initial difficulties with a breaking rope, but then it was
doubled, and after much heaving and straining, the
statue began to move. The enthusiastic islanders yelled
at the tops of their voices, and Thor Heyerdahl tells us
that soon the stone statue was moving as easily as if it
had been an empty soap box.

Von Daniken had written in *Chariots of the Gods?*:
"The usual explanation, that the stone giants were
moved to their present sites on wooden rollers, is not
feasible in this case, either." [9]

Thor Heyerdahl showed that rollers were not required, but that good strong ropes were. Rope making has been one of man's earliest achievements, and the fertile soil of Easter Island could produce the required materials.

Thor Heyerdahl had answered a number of questions posed by Erich Von Daniken before they were asked:

> Then who cut the statues out of the rock, who carved them and transported them to their sites? How were they moved across country for miles without rollers? How were they dressed, polished, and erected? How were the hats, the stones which came from a different quarry from that of the statues, put in place? . . . Even 2,000 men, working day and night, would not be nearly enough to carve these colossal figures out of the steel-hard volcanic stone with rudimentary tools . . .[10]

## The Chariots Still Crash

Von Daniken did not concede that the Easter Islanders could have completed the statue they began for Heyerdahl, and he tells us, "We, too, bashed away at the rock like wild men, using the biggest stones we could find. After a few hundred blows, there was nothing left of our tools but a few miserable splinters, but the rock showed hardly a scratch."[11] However, "bashing away" is the wrong method. If his men had used the flaking action required, they might have accomplished more.

In his second book he acknowledged that "after Heyerdahl's successful experiment, I was quite prepared to cross an unsolved puzzle off my list as solved."[12] He then had second thoughts, acknowledging only that "the stone-tool theory may be valid for some of the smaller statues which originated in an age nearer our own . . ."[13] He does acknowledge that "Heyerdahl erected a medium-sized statue by means of wooden beams and a primitive but successful technique, and then moved it with the help of ropes and about a hundred men on the heave-ho principle." [14] This is interesting to put alongside one of Von Daniken's earlier statements which specifically states that the "heave-ho" method would have been impossible on Easter Island for lack of manpower.[15]

Heave-ho! It certainly will require a lot of manpower to pull out another Von Daniken chariot that has gone crashing into those mysterious rock craters on Easter Island.

Von Daniken himself states: "Perhaps it seems presumptuous of me . . . to reject Heyerdahl's theory," and he goes on, "here is my explanation—as usual, one that seems fantastic." [16] We agree. It *does* seem presumptuous, and his "stranded astronauts" theory *is* fantastic. We go along with Thor Heyerdahl.

One last point. Erich Von Daniken himself tells us, "On Easter Island the gods were worshipped as lords of space." [17] It appears that even the direction in which the statues were positioned on the cliff's edge was part of that worship. This is the same pattern seen at so many ancient sites—no effort was spared to please the gods of the sky who were so important for the fertility of crops and animals alike.

We conclude, then, that the patterns of sudden appearance, similarity of language, and huge constructions dedicated to the gods of the sky, as seen on Easter Island, have similarities to many other civilizations of the past.

## CHAPTER 4

# Dating the Rocks—
# or Rocking the Dates?

As I have traveled in various parts of the world, especially across the U.S.A. and in my own land of Australia, I have found that many people are seriously interested in the accuracy or otherwise of Carbon-14 dating, and of other systems that are similar in their basic assumptions. Carbon dating has engendered much popular interest, and people are greatly interested in the so-called scientific method of dating.

As this new system is highly relevant in a book dealing with ancient civilizations, we shall pause to consider its merits.

It is worth noting that there have also been other dating methods, and some of these are still widely used. Estimates of the time required to cool the earth's crust, the rate of change of igneous rocks into sedimentary rocks, the rate at which salt is carried into the ocean, the possible age of meteorites, calculations involving astronomy—these are but some of the dating methods utilized by scientists. Clearly, not all the relevant assumptions involve radioactivity.

## Geological Dating Is Suspect

Another widely discussed dating method is that of the geologists as they estimate the age of the earth's strata. These scientists usually presume that geological changes continue to be brought about by the same forces that led to similar changes in past ages. It is presumed that the changes are taking place now as they always have done: this is a form of uniformitarianism.

In the geological strata it is presumed that the lower deposits are older than those at the higher levels. Also,

if there is an igneous intrusion that cuts across the geological layer, this so-called sike is reckoned as younger
than the layer that surrounds it. However, this "parent-
daughter" relationship does not always fit.

Another point is that rocks are presumed to be the
same age as fossils found in those rocks, having been
laid down at the same time. Then, by circular reasoning, it is also decided that the fossils are the same age
as the rocks. Thus, speaking generally, the geologists
look to the biologists, and the biologists accept the
geologists' virtual infallibility, with neither school sufficiently realizing the circularity involved. The assumption is made that rocks with similar fossils, in any part
of the earth, will be virtually the same age.

Although these assumptions cannot be proved, and
in fact have been disproved from time to time, they are
still vociferously supported. The so-called geological
column of the earth's strata is a theoretical concept—it
would require a hundred miles of strata to demonstrate
it, and the deepest site available (the Grand Canyon
in Colorado) offers only a fraction of that. In any case,
the evidence in the "new world" often differs from
what had been apparently established in the "old
world." Dating of fossils by rocks, and rocks by fossils,
is demonstrably unreliable.

## Tree Rings Are Sometimes Unreliable

Another problem related to dating is that of esti-
mating a tree's age by its seasonal rings. It is sometimes
claimed that measuring time by counting the annual
tree rings correlates well with Carbon-14 datings, but
tree-ring measurement is not entirely satisfactory. In
irregular years there can be two rainy seasons, and this
would produce two rings instead of one.

In fact, under certain conditions a tree may demonstrate even more than two rings in a year. Three is not
uncommon, as with a tree that grows on a slope. If the

water supply runs off rapidly it sometimes gives an artificial wet and dry period three or more times in a year. There are even cases where the opposite sides of a tree have exhibited different numbers of rings. Thus correlations between tree rings and C-14 dates can at best be only a general guide.

Erich Von Daniken has an interesting example to show that dating by tree rings might give a drastically different age from that arrived at by the C-14 method:

> If grasses and bushes on the edge of a highway are cut and burned, the ashes give a false age of many thousands of years. Why is that? Day after day, the plants have absorbed large amounts of carbon petroleum, but that in turn comes from organic material that stopped absorbing C-14 from the atmosphere millions of years ago. Thus a tree cut down in an industrial district may be only fifty years old according to its annual rings, but examinations by the C-14 method would date the wood ash so far back that the fifty-year-old tree would have had to have been planted in very remote times.[1]

Von Daniken goes on to state that he doubts the accuracy of this method, and points out that the measurements "start from the firm assumption that the proportion of a C-14 isotope in the atmosphere is and was always the same. But who knows if that is true?"[2] Although in other places Von Daniken is happy enough to accept Carbon-14 dating,[3] he is right in this question. The constancy of C-14 is not assured, as we shall see.

## The New Methods and Radioactivity

What then of the new methods, based on radio-activity? First, we should briefly outline what "carbon dating" is.

It was made public in 1949 by Dr. W. F. Libby. He

showed that all living cells have the same specific radio-activity because of the presence of approximately 765 atoms of Carbon-14 for every billion atoms of Carbon-12. Carbon-12 is constant in a living organism, but Carbon-14 is absorbed during life, then slowly given off after the organism has died.

Put simply, all living things are absorbing and dis-charging radioactive Carbon-14 at a uniform rate. When an organism dies, there is no longer any intake of Carbon-14 isotopes, and those that remain break down very slowly. By measurement of this "residue," the Carbon-14 dating method claims to find approximately when a thing was actually living. Half of the radioactive Carbon-14 disintegrates in approximately 5,700 years, then half of the remainder is discharged in the next 5,700 years, and the theory is that this continues at a uniform rate. This means that after about 34,000 years the measurable Carbon-14 isotopes still existing would be only 1/64 as compared with when the organism died. The Carbon-14 present can be calculated with a Geiger counter. The count per minute of the beta rays given off indicates whether there is high or low radio-activity.

Carbon dating offers real possibilities for dating, at least for one half-life. However, there are serious prob-lems. One basic assumption is that it is known what the initial conditions were when the radioactivity began. As this cannot be known with certainty, we again have a measure of circularity. The starting conditions must be postulated, and then the calculated age is dependent on those assumed starting conditions.

## Assumptions That Cannot Be Verified

There are a number of other assumptions relative to Carbon-14 dating that cannot be verified, including the following:

1. That the sample is sufficiently pure and pre-

served from leaching, incident of radiation, etc.

2. That the amount of C-14 in the biosphere has remained essentially the same through time. This is in turn dependent on three supposedly independent geophysical qualities—

   (a) The average cosmic ray intensity over a period of 8,000 years (average radio carbon life).

   (b) Magnetic field magnitude in earth's vicinity, averaged over the same period.

   (c) The degree of mixing of the earth's oceans during the same period of time.

3. The constancy of nonradioactive $CO_2$ in the atmosphere. If it were as high as .3 percent in the past instead of .03 percent, there would be 10 times more C-12 in relation to C-14 as there is observed today; plants and animals would contain 10 times less C-14 to begin with than they do today, and their apparent ages would be much older than their true ages correspondingly.[4]

The formation of C-14 depends on cosmic rays, these being charged particles that are in rapid motion. Carbon-14 is one of the substances formed when nitrogen is broken down by the force of cosmic radiation. As cosmic rays approach the magnetic field of the earth they can be deflected from the direction of their previous motion, and a fraction of them will be so deflected so that they will not enter the earth's atmosphere. The actual fraction will depend on the strength of the earth's magnetic field, and it is known that this has decreased over recent centuries—the earth's magnetic field is not constant, and neither are the cosmic rays. Both could have been stronger or weaker at various times in the past—no one knows, and this means that C-14 data will not be absolute. Corrections are necessary because of the inherent possibility of error in the system.

Solar activity of various types—e.g., flares and sun-spots—can dramatically alter the level of radioactivity, and it is impossible to know just what effect this has had on dating. It is also conceded that the so-called Ice Age might have caused major variations in the amount of radio-carbon activity.

## Some Surprising Results of Carbon Dating

When carbon dating was first announced by Dr. Libby in 1949 it was thought to be the last word, but that early confidence has been replaced by a sense of caution—as Dr. Libby himself has testified.

Robert L. Whitelaw, Professor of Nuclear and Mechanical Engineering at the Virginia Polytechnic Institute in Blacksburg, Virginia, wrote in 1970 that ninety-one universities and laboratories in twenty-five different countries had dated more than 15,000 specimens of once-living matter in the twenty years since carbon dating had been introduced.[5] Dr. Whitelaw collected many of these test results, and there are some surprising facts. Practically every specimen of once living material is found to be datable within 50,000 years.[6] There is one sample of fossil coal dated to only 4,250 years ago, with another sample of coal being even younger—1,680 years old.

One of the few skulls shown as more than 50,000 years was the so-called Neanderthal skeleton in the Shanidar 1 Cave in Iraq—its given date was 50,600. The Keilor Skull, found at Keilor just outside Melbourne in Victoria, was dated to 8,500. This is much more recent than the 150,000 years that traditional dating had demanded. Even relatively recent dates such as 8,000 and 10,000 are not necessarily to be accepted, according to Dr. Whitelaw, and possibly the figures should be considerably lower. In any case, by far the greatest proportion of Carbon-14 dates are within about the last 6,000 years.

Dr. Whitelaw discusses Professor Libby's conclusions and his later concessions as to the errors within the original hypotheses, and then Whitelaw comes up with a series of correlations. His proposals for new dates are reasonably close to the published C-14 dates up to 5,000 years, but beyond that time his suggestions drastically shorten the published ages. The published C-14 age of 5,990 years would be 5,000 years; 8,860 years would be 5,500 years; 12,530 years would be 6,000 years; 19,100 years would be 6,500 years; and "infinite" would actually be 7,000 years. However, Dr. Whitelaw's suggestions are tentative only.

Nevertheless there is compelling evidence to look again at these "long" ages. Carbon-14 dates have been obtained for both coal and oil—a subject on which we shall elaborate. If they were millions of years old, as usually accepted, they should not give a measurement by the C-14 method.

## The Flood and Atmospheric Changes

To explain that and related points, we need first to consider a number of issues involving the possibility of a global flood. This is not necessarily a matter of faith: many "Bible believers" believe in a so-called local flood, confined to the Euphrates-Tigris Basin. Others insist on a universal deluge. We are not debating the issue as such except insofar as it is relevant to Carbon-14 dating.

If the Bible record and worldwide traditions are to be taken seriously there could have been great atmospheric changes, such as that the present cosmic ray activity might well have been screened out from the earth before that time.

With necessary refinements to the system, carbon dating offers possibilities for approximate dating for as long ago as one half-life of about 5,700 years. Beyond that we have no absolutes, such as written records, with which to compare the given dates.

This record of a universal flood is known in many records outside the Bible, although Professor W. F. Albright pointed out that the Bible record contains archaic features, and it dates before any Mesopotamian version preserved in cuneiform sources.[7] The possibility of such an inundation is taken seriously by reputable scholars.

Robert T. Boyd has an interesting statement:

> There are no less than 330 separate racial records among people and races who are living today. . . . "Fa-ha," whom the Chinese say is their founder, is represented as having escaped with his wife, three sons and three daughters from a flood that was sent "because man rebelled against heaven." The English, Hindus, Aztecs of Mexico, Incas of Peru, the Fiji Islanders, and even the American Indians have traditional stories about a flood.[8]

Robert Boyd goes on to discuss a very interesting Polynesian account of the flood which at some points is remarkably similar to the record in Genesis.

Studies made during the 1957–58 International Geophysical Year indicated there was a tendency for carbon dioxide in the atmosphere to so increase that by the year 2000 it would be 30 percent greater than at present, brought about by industrial pollution of the atmosphere itself. Professor Alceo Magnanini, Director of the Tijica National Park near Rio de Janerio, suggested that if this pollution overcame the controlling role of forests and plants there would be a consequent rise in the temperature of the earth's atmosphere, and the ice caps would be melted. This, he claimed, would lead to a rise of about sixty-five feet in the level of the oceans, and cities such as New York and Paris could be wiped out.

This might seem somewhat dramatic, but the Bible record and the many traditions around the world indicate widespread belief that such a catastrophe has already taken place once in man's relatively recent history.

## Oil and Coal Formed Recently?

Some scholars go even further and suggest that this is the time when the great oil deposits of the earth were formed. If it covered all the high mountains of the world, a universal flood would involve water to a depth of six miles. As most fish are limited as to possible migration, and as 90 percent of them live in the first fifty fathoms of the ocean depths, such a greatly increased volume of water would lead to tremendous pressure on them. Obviously vast quantities of fish would die, and it is seriously argued by some scholars that this accounts for large deposits of oil.

We have seen that some carbon datings point to the relatively recent formation of coal and oil: we suggested that the very fact that coal and oil can show the presence of C-14 is a significant pointer to their recency.[9]

This problem of dating leads into many diverse channels, touching again and again on concepts that a generation ago seemed to be nicely settled. We have touched on oil, and the same arguments can be advanced concerning coal. Even human skeletons have been found in coal. Somewhat less grisly was the widely reported incident in 1891 when a woman in Morrisonville, Illinois, accidentally dropped a shovelful of coal on the floor. One of the large pieces broke open, revealing an eight-carat gold chain, ten inches long, coiled and embedded inside. The coal broke into two pieces, and the two ends of the chain remained attached, one to each of the different fragments.

Other metal objects, and even an iron pot, have been found embedded in lumps of coal. The significance of these findings is that they demonstrate that man and his handmade implements were on the earth before the coal itself was formed.[10]

## Coal and Fossils Both Formed Rapidly

It is now believed that coal is formed rapidly—in fact, if it is not formed rapidly it does not form at all. Trees or plant debris need to be buried, compressed, and cut off from oxidation. Thus it is that some highly reputable scholars believe that the great coal beds were formed at the time of the universal flood. Although this argument is not accepted by all, it is a reasonable explanation—that coal beds formed when great quantities of plant matter were washed together, and were then quickly covered by layers of mud, sand, and debris. Proponents of this theory point out that under more normal conditions the plant matter would soon decay and merely rot into humus.[11]

An alternative sometimes put forward to explain the formation of coal is the so-called peat-bog theory, but peat is never found in layers of more than a few feet. This could not be the answer to coal seams that are found all around the world, nor is there evidence that present-day peat is changing into coal. The largest coal seams are about 100 times larger than could be expected from the most substantial peat-bog.

The argument for recency can also be put forward about fossils. These are the hard parts of plants or animals that have been preserved in a petrified form in rocks. Imprints in soft mud can be formed in the same way—they can be hardened into rock provided they are suddenly covered as the result of something like a volcanic eruption or a sudden flood. For the fossil to be formed, the plant or animal covered by water needs to be cut off suddenly by a layer such as clay. It must then be undisturbed, sealed off, for a long process of petrification.

There are other serious problems about "long" dating—such as the relative lack of sediments if the oceans are billions of years old, as we often read. The return of ocean sediments back to the continents has been shown as not the answer. "Sea-floor spreading" is also not the solution, for "ocean sediments are forming today at a rate ten times faster than they are being destroyed by sea-floor spreading." [12]

## The Tendency to Recency

We have seen that Carbon-14 has involved a tendency toward recency in dating, leading to a serious revision of many previously accepted dates. Another example is the so-called Talgai Skull, found near Talgai in Southern Queensland, Australia, in 1886. Instead of being hundreds of thousands of years old, the skull was dated as 13,000 years old. There have been other embarrassing changes—one famous example was a civilization in Mesopotamia that was supposedly hundreds of thousands of years old, but then a flat-bottomed boat, which could not have been more than 5,000 years old, was found at a lower level. This meant that the supposed prehistoric level was relatively modern. These are not isolated incidents.

It happens that Erich Von Daniken has come to the conclusion that Carbon-14 is unreliable, and in his third book, *The Gold of the Gods* he tells us:

> At a chemical congress in Los Angeles, Dr. John Lynde Anderson of Chattanooga, Tennessee, explained that his experiments with the radioactive carbon isotope C-14 had produced deviations from the results which should be obtained according to the theory. To make sure he repeated his experiments with different equipment and on hundreds of organic objects, yet even on one and the same object the results were different.
>
> Archaeologists still look on the C-14 method as

the only canonised process for dating artefacts. How can people be so blind and stubborn? [13]

It is nonsense to suggest that archaeologists look on the C-14 method as "canonized," but it is a fact that this system has been widely accepted in a way that the results do not justify. Dates given by the C-14 method have indicated much younger ages than were expected by the testers.

## The Rocks Are Apparently Young After All

On the other hand, some dates obtained by other radiometric methods are seriously astray in the opposite direction, such as an age of millions of years being attributed to volcanic rocks in Hawaii which are known to be less than 200 years old.

This is reported in the *Journal of Geophysical Research*.[14] It is known that these lava rocks were actually formed in 1800 and 1801 in Hualalai in Hawaii. The potassium-argon dating method was utilized, and a formation age of 160 million to 3 billion years was given for this rock formation known to be just over 170 years old. This is not an isolated report, as this quotation indicates:

> Rock samples from 12 volcanoes in Russia and 10 samples from other places around the world, all known to be of recent age (formed within the last 200 years), when dated by the uranium-thorium-lead method gave ages varying from millions to billions of years! [15]

The continuing evidence has led to caution in scientific circles toward such methods as the potassium to argon, and uranium to lead processes whereby the ages of rocks have been calculated.

Dr. L. Hallonquist discusses reports that have been presented by prestigious bodies or journals around the world, including the *Journal of Geophysical Research, Science, The Geological Institute, The Academy of*

*Science, U.S.S.R.,* and others. Such reports have originated from Norway, Germany, France, Holland, the United States, and other countries. Dr. Hallonquist then makes this statement:

> The startling fact now coming to light, namely, that the daughter isotopes or elements on which the dates are calculated, instead of being accumulated in the rocks over long periods of time during the decay of the parent radioactive material, entered the rocks at the time of their formation from the liquid magma, is indeed devastating to the whole system of radiometric rock dating. The new findings strike at the very heart of radiometric systems of rock dating and make them worthless. In fact, if taken to their logical conclusion, these new results indicate a relatively young age, of at the most a few thousand years, for all rocks, instead of the extreme billions of years previously postulated.[16]

This is a serious blow to accepted dating systems. Dr. Hallonquist's use of terms such as "devastating" and "worthless" might seem extreme, but the fact is that radiometric dating has posed serious problems and has led to dramatic changing of many dates.

## Carbon Dates on Dr. Leakey's Finds

Another example of change is that of the bones found by Dr. Louis Leakey in the Olduvai Gorge in Kenya, Africa, which gave an age of 10,100 years instead of the 2,000,000 years that Dr. Leakey had hoped for.[17]

Leakey's famous *Zinjanthropus,* from that same Olduvai Gorge, was dated by the potassium-argon method at 1,750,000 years. However, other bones from the same bed were given a C-14 test, and the date was 10,000 years.[18] Dr. Whitelaw points out that in the journal *Science* the frank admission was made that there was a serious problem of relating to the dating of Bed I in the Olduvai Gorge where Leakey's fossil *Zinjanthropus* was found.[19]

The work of Dr. Louis Leakey has been carried on by his son Richard Leakey, and he in turn has found other skulls. In a public lecture in San Diego he claimed that what he had found destroyed all that had ever been taught about human evolution. He is quoted as saying, "I have nothing to offer in its place." [20] He makes a similar statement in the *National Geographic* magazine of June, 1973.

Richard Leakey is not the only one to recognize problems as to early man and dating sequences. In fact, there have been great changes in classifications of prehistoric man. Neanderthal man has been reclassified as Homo sapiens, the classification of modern man, as shown by the recent replacements in the Chicago Museum of Natural History. So-called Nebraska man was put to one side because it was found that his whole reconstruction was based on a prehistoric pig's tooth; then *Zinjanthropus,* the East Africa man of Dr. Leakey, was also put to one side. Now Richard Leakey is putting forward his viewpoint, and many anthropologists and other scientists are taking seriously his claims that other so-called prehistoric men were not in a direct line to modern man. One basic problem is that new skull findings often prove to be younger (more recent) than modern men—that is, the supposed parents were younger than the children.

It has also been realized that some of the "early men" differed from modern man only in that they had congenital defects, or had suffered from arthritis or a bone disease through their lifetime.

## Humans and Dinosaurs Together?

Another serious dating problem relates to the finding of what appear to be both human and dinosaur footprints, virtually next to each other in cretaceous rock, found in the bed of the Paluxy River at Glen Rose in Texas.[21] An attempt was made to explain these markings as due to erosion, but actually erosion would help to destroy such prints.

I have seen the colored movie *Footprints in Stone* dealing with these finds, and, to say the least, it is thought-provoking. It is very difficult to believe that what are clearly giant human footsteps were made in any other way than by a human being. When it is then established that a dinosaur track is in the same vicinity, at one point passing only seventeen inches from the human footprint, it is difficult to explain according to traditional dates given for prehistoric monsters such as dinosaurs. Unpalatable as such a possibility is to a number of branches of science, it begins to seem that early man and prehistoric animals were here at the same time.

All this is tied up with radio-carbon dating and other radiometric systems: there is increasing evidence to suggest that those figures of millions of years which we were given in our childhood must be put to one side. Even if the dates determined by radiometric processes are accepted without modification, it is yet true that those processes have consistently reduced the long time periods widely accepted a generation ago for man and past civilizations.

## Population Points to Man's Recency

Another interesting point relating to the flood is put forward by Professor H. Enoch. He states that statisticians agree that 150 years is a reasonable average to assume for population to double itself, having made allowance for wars, famines, etc. He shows that from the time of the biblical Jacob until 1930 (before Hitler's massacre of millions of Jews) the Jewish people doubled approximately once every 161 years. If we accept Bible dates, and that Noah and his family were the only humans alive after the flood, the population of 2,500 million in 1966 could have been reached by a doubling process every 160 years. Professor Enoch has a suggested date of 2519 B.C. for the deluge.[22]

We are not accepting this argument in its entirety, for it is not entirely "waterproof," in that some contingencies can only be guessed at—as Professor Enoch himself allows: e.g., that Hitler's massacres must be judged "exceptional," and that plagues, etc., could also have decimated populations. Nevertheless, the argument is a pointer toward recency of population, and toward the possibility that there was such a worldwide catastrophe. In fact, there appears to be no convincing argument *against* recency.

The world's population does seem to indicate the recency of man, as shown by the following calculation:

If every family had on the average four children, who live on the average of two generations, in only 30 generations of 35 years per generation we would have the present world population of 3.2 billion persons—in just 1,050 years! If there were only 3 children per family, each child living only one generation, we have in 1,820 years (52 generations) 4.34 billion people. For an average family of 2.5 children, with $x = 1$, and a generation being 43 years on an average, the present population would be generated in 100 generations, or 4,300 years.

On the other hand, if man is about half a million years old, the present population should stand at roughly $10^{500}$, an incredible number of 10 followed by 500 zeros, if $x = 1$, and there are 3 children per family. Since a maximum of $10^{100}$ bodies could be packed into the known Universe, some evolutionary estimates are rather obviously way out! The present population could only have

been produced by a few thousand years of multi-
plication, even with large allowances for population decimation and very limited averages per
family and generation.[23]

## Carbon Dioxide ... Tomatoes ... and Long-Living Men!

Indirectly, even the concept of men living for very
long periods of time is involved with that Flood. Other
peoples also had such traditions, though they were
greatly exaggerated when compared with the biblical
figures.

Dr. George Howe has a relevant comment. It is
rather complex, but for the sake of what follows we
give it in full:

Now, let's suppose there was the same absolute
amount of C-14 in the air before the Flood as
now. But if there were a much greater amount of
C-12 before the Flood, the ratio of C-14 to C-12
would be smaller. After the Flood there would be
a higher ratio of C-14 because possibly more of
the C-12 was removed from the earth's cycle in
forming vast coal deposits and fossil beds. Thus
the Flood might have changed the carbon economy
and the ratios considerably. This would also mean
that there would be a much higher ratio of C-14
to C-12 after the Flood. Thus, a bone formed
before the Flood would possibly have less C-14
per gram of C-12 than one formed after the
Flood because of the greater amount of C-12 in
the atmosphere before the Flood.[24]

One practical application of this is illustrated by Dr.
Howe: "A friend of mine found that if he put 10 times
the usual amount of carbon dioxide in the air, his
tomatoes would grow and produce much better than in
normal air."

It is interesting to pose a question: if there was more

C-12 in the air before the Flood than there is now, is this part of the explanation as to why, both in the Bible and in other ancient records, we read of men living for hundreds of years? Obviously the thousands of years referred to in the Kish King List are embellishments, for there we read of kings who lived for periods ranging through 10,800 to 64,800 years. By comparison the biblical dates of 800 and 900 years are conservative. In view of the above argument from well-nourished tomatoes, possibly the change in the earth's atmosphere is a pointer to how men could live longer "before the Flood."

## A Water Vapor Around the Earth?

It is even possible there was a water vapor blanket around the earth until the time of that Flood. Such a theory is put forward seriously by competent men of science—as in one of the papers submitted in January, 1970, to the Lunar Science Conference at Houston, Texas.

Dr. A. E. Ringwood reported that his investigation of lunar rock samples indicates that most of the accepted theories about the origin of the moon were wrong.[25] Part of Dr. Ringwood's conclusion was that early in the earth's history it had a massive atmosphere, at a high enough temperature to evaporate certain elements that were being collected by the earth's movement through space.

Dr. Ringwood was not identifying this with the Flood, but it could be relevant to that happening. The fact is, the possibility of an atmospheric envelope should be taken seriously. This also might be relevant to the concept of long-living men discussed above, in that the nonpenetration of our atmosphere by dangerous ultraviolet and other rays would make longer life possible.

In addition, the sudden death of animals in areas

such as Siberia, with large quantities of undigested tropical food in their stomachs, points to a dramatic climatic change, possibly this also being the time of the Flood. An atmospheric canopy such as Dr. Ringwood proposed would have given the world a uniform climate, and it appears to have had such a climate, judging by tropical flora recently recovered in the Antarctic. These various evidences point to dramatic changes in climatic conditions, and they could be tied in to the biblical Flood.

## In Conclusion

It appears that dramatic changes occurred in the earth's atmosphere a few thousand years ago. Beyond that time—roughly one half-life of Carbon-14—radiometric dating is not reliable.

According to Dr. George Howe, the scientists who actually perform the analysis to estimate the C-14 per unit of total carbon left in the bone do not give specific dates beyond 3,000 years. Some scientists who use the method will propose dates extending back 50,000 years and even further, but "the men who know the limits of the method, the men who run the tests, would report that they cannot date with accuracy beyond 3,000 years." [26]

Speaking generally, there is a measure of consistency with Carbon-14 dates that involve less than one half-life, though even in that period considerable correction is at times required.

The basic assumptions on which carbon dating was based have been set aside as constants—they are variables after all, though possibly acceptable as approximations. Even the strength of the earth's magnetic field, previously supposed to be a constant, extends considerably far out into space, and varies in intensity: it is a variable, not a constant. Nor has the carbon dioxide content of the atmosphere been constant through the ages.

The sunspot cycle that takes place every eleven years has an effect on the number of cosmic rays reaching the earth, and solar flares that burst out of the sun's surface also produce Carbon-14. Thus the supply of Carbon-14 is virtually unpredictable. An extensive solar flare can produce as much Carbon-14 in a few minutes as would be produced by the more usual solar activity in a whole year.

The fact is, radio chronologists have no solid basis for determining the ages of rocks or anything else beyond the absolutes of written records that extend over only a few thousand years. The assumptions behind these dating methods are now highly questionable, and the flow of evidence has demonstrated that radiometric dating, which offered such great potentiality, is certainly not infallible. Despite modifications, many scientists are by no means as sure about the new dating systems as they were twenty years ago.

## CHAPTER 5

# Stonehenge: The Magic of Merlin, or the Men from Mars?

We have suggested that with necessary modifications carbon dating will prove to be important for approximately as far back as 5,000 years, where dates can be compared with absolutes such as written records. In this chapter we shall relate that possibility to another series of monuments from the past. We refer to Stonehenge in England, another mystery of previous ages that Erich Von Daniken links into his way-out system. He talks about ancient peoples apparently taking special pleasure in juggling huge stone giants over the hills and valleys.

> The Egyptians fetched their obelisk from Aswan, the architects of Stonehenge brought their stone blocks from southwest Wales and Marlborough, the stonemasons of Easter Island took their ready-made monster statues from a distant quarry to their present sites, and no one can say where some of the monoliths at Tiahuanaco come from.[1]

## Those Unknown Space Travelers Again

Von Daniken makes much of these seemingly strange activities around the world and tells us that "our remote ancestors must have been strange people; they liked making things difficult for themselves and always built their statues in the most impossible places." He suggests that this was not simply because they liked the hard life. He refuses to believe that the artists of ancient times would have been as stupid as that: they could have erected their temples and statues much nearer the quarries if it had not been for traditions that stated where the buildings must be located.

He then talks about "the unknown space travelers who visited our planet many thousands of years ago," who would not have been less far-sighted than we are today. All this is tied up, so we are told, with man's ultimate task of colonizing the universe, when ultimately the promise of the gods will be realized and peace will come on earth. According to Von Daniken, the sites chosen for these great statues and monoliths are relevant for the "further development of present-day space travel." [2]

A number of these ancient buildings were associated with men worshipping the heavenly bodies and the gods who were supposed to live on them. However, we need not accept the wild hypothesis of Erich Von Daniken about space visitors to believe that moon worship and various forms of superstitious idolatry were indulged in by men of old. The Babylonians, the Assyrians, the Chinese, and many other ancient civilizations did their utmost to placate the gods. With many people this especially involved fertility rites. To ensure that crops would flourish, priests engaged in sexual practices with animals. At times human sacrifices were also offered, and many other weird rites were carried out.

## The Monuments and the Seasons

In ancient times the sun's seasonal movements were widely known, and simple astronomical devices were developed whereby men could anticipate such important happenings as the summer and winter solstices.

We suggested that many of the great monuments of the past are found to have some association with the seasons, and Stonehenge is apparently in this category. These massive megaliths stand on the Salisbury Plain of Wiltshire in the south of England, and archaeologists believe they have been there for nearly 4,000 years. It seems probable that they were not suddenly erected in a very brief period, but that building extended over 300 or 400 years. Some additions were apparently made at an even later time. The dates cannot be established certainly, but as far as Britain was concerned this was the so-called Neolithic Age—the "New Stone Age." This means that the original workers were "Stone Age Men," and would have been restricted to the implements and methodology associated with such an age.

## Temples Before Stonehenge in Britain?

No one really knows when the building of ancient temples in Britain was commenced, but a number of Carbon-14 dates are available.[3] The altar at Stonehenge—possibly a very late addition—is given as only $1,846\pm275$ years old (i.e., about 100 A.D.), but no doubt many of the structures at this site were considerably earlier. The Carbon-14 date for the pyramid mound at Avebury, only seventeen miles from Stonehenge, is $4,115\pm95$ years—about 2100 B.C. It is believed that this site originally consisted of about 650 huge stones. It was apparently the oldest of the early centers, but it is not as well preserved as Stonehenge. It is possible that the structures at both Avebury and Stonehenge were being built as long ago as the time of Abraham (about 2000 B.C.), though it might be that only the Avebury constructions were erected so early and that the nearby cultic centers of Stonehenge and Woodhenge followed later. Woodhenge was two miles northeast of Stonehenge.

Referring to the huge pyramids and religious structures in so many parts of the world, Charles Berlitz points out:

> It is a matter of conjecture whether these enormous mounds were inspired by a common source such as Sumeria, Egypt, or even an earlier culture that has disappeared, or were simply the

result of a shared natural urge to build a lasting tomb, or to set up a temple "in the high places" connected with sun worship or astronomy.[4]

Is it even possible that that common origin is linked with the dispersion that the Bible talks about, at the time of the building of the Tower of Babel?

## The Early Builders of Stonehenge

It is usually agreed that the first building period of Stonehenge itself was somewhere about 1800 B.C., when the original circle of stones was erected. This was followed by a second phase, lasting about 150 to 250 years from 1650 B.C., involving the erection of a large number of bluestones in a circle around the center. These bluestone rocks had to be transported from the Prescelly Mountains of Pembrokeshire in the southwest of Wales, hauled across country, and then transported down the Avon River. From their landing point they must have been dragged some two miles from the river to Stonehenge itself.

Like so many others, these structures might be associated with an even earlier civilization, for nobody really knows the date when the massive stones were put into place. Although round figures of 1800 B.C. to 1400 B.C. are given for Stonehenge, we do not really know the actual time of its construction. If dating becomes more precise, we might be surprised to find fascinating synchronizations between many of these ancient temples in so-called old and new lands alike.

In the meantime, however, we do have certain clues. In 1901 the British Astronomer Royal, Sir Norman Lockyer, related astronomical movements to the positions of the Stonehenge monoliths, and calculated that the date of construction was between 1900 and 1500 B.C. His calculations have been challenged at a number of points, but an independent assessment indicates that possibly the date itself was somewhere near the mark.

A carbon date was obtained for a sample of charcoal from one of the Aubrey Holes—which we shall explain later in this chapter—and it gave a date of 1848 B.C.± 275 years. This is reasonably close to the date that Lockyer had calculated.

It seems too much of a coincidence that Avebury, Stonehenge, and Woodhenge—within a radius of twenty miles—would have been totally unrelated. It is far more likely that there were close religious ties. We have seen that a carbon date of about 2100 B.C. has been obtained from Avebury, and that is virtually the same date that Professor W. F. Albright suggested for the Tower of Babel incident—as we saw in our discussion about Easter Island.

Once again, did a number of men obey some inner compulsion—a compulsion they could not refuse? Why did they voyage across the sea to Britain, that island whose importance was to be far greater than they ever anticipated? It is at least thought-provoking that yet another time clue could lead us back to that same incident of the Tower of Babel.

## The Reconstruction of Stonehenge

Stonehenge itself is not as impressive as the pyramids or, for example, the Roman Colosseum, but it is still remarkable. It is surrounded by a ditch, with a bank of earth thrown up around most of its circumference of 320 feet. Within this circle of earth there are fifty-six pits, rediscovered in the seventeenth century A.D. by John Aubrey, hence the modern name of "Aubrey Holes." Some of the holes were probably dug for wooden poles, others to hold stones upright. In a number of the holes bones of cremated human beings were found, and the theory was propagated that the pits must have been a necropolis. However, the evidence is not conclusive, and though it seems probable that the holes

had some religious significance, the details are uncertain.

There are many hewn monumental stones about
thirty feet high, some still erect, but others have fallen.
Unlike the pyramids that had to be uncovered from the
dust, sand, and dirt that had blown in over the centuries, Stonehenge did not have to be rediscovered. It
has been part of England's silent history for thousands
of years. It has not always been "guarded" history—
even in the eighteenth century it was possible to hire
hammers at a nearby town to break off souvenir pieces!

Restoration work by the British government has
made it possible to get a reasonably accurate idea of
what the original Stonehenge must have looked like.

## A Description of Stonehenge

From where the stones had to be dragged from the
Avon River two miles away, an avenue was formed.
This led up to the "Heel Stone" (sometimes spelt with
the Old English form, "hele"), about seventy-five feet
to the northeast of the ditch and the earthwork sur-
rounding Stonehenge itself. It is called "Heel Stone"
because the shape of its base is somewhat like a heel.

Proceeding past the Heel Stone, down the avenue,
and across the ditch area, one comes to the site of the
slaughter stones. These lay at the entrance to the outer
circle, but only one of the stones is still at this position.
They more or less formed an entrance gateway through
the outer circle that comprised a rampart and a ditch.
After passing through the "Aubrey Holes," one moves
on toward the inner series of circles and horseshoes.
First there was the so-called Sarsen Circle, consisting
of thirty huge sandstone monoliths, and seventeen of
the original thirty stones are still in position. These
stones are about fourteen feet high, and they originally
came from the Marlborough Downs about twenty miles
away. They are gray sandstone, and the word "sarsen"

comes from "saracen" which means "something foreign."

Inside the Sarsen Circle was another circle, this time of bluestones, and inside that again were two horseshoe structures—the Sarsen Horseshoe and the Bluestone Horseshoe. Finally, in front of the Bluestone Horseshoe, what was apparently the Altar Stone was located, but it is no longer standing. It is conjectured to have been an altar stone because of the belief that Stonehenge was a sacred sanctuary. Not all scholars accept this identification of an altar, and we saw that a carbon date from this area suggested 100 A.D., which is many hundreds of years younger than the usually accepted dates for the Stonehenge monoliths.

This "Altar Stone" was made of sandstone, though apparently not of the variety that came from the Marlborough Downs—it is conjectured that it came from Milford Haven, on the seacoast of southwestern Wales.

There were also four series of circular holes, known as Y and Z holes, and Q and R holes. The Y and Z holes were between the Aubrey Holes and the Sarsen Circle. The Q holes—about six feet apart—were between the Sarsen Circle and the Bluestone Circle, while the R holes, also about six feet apart, were between the Bluestone Circle and the Sarsen Horseshoe.

## Primitive Tools and Ancient Builders

The whole structure is fantastic when we consider the primitive tools of crude stone and wood that were available. Even the "crowbars" must have been timber braced against timber, thus making leverage possible. The builders probably constructed ramps of earth so that the great lintel stones which formed a circle across the top could be hoisted into position.

Archaeologists have been able to understand some of the processes because of the evidence found in the stones themselves, such as protruding tenons from one stone fitting neatly into a prepared hole in the stone above it.

Charles Berlitz has an interesting comment as to the possible relationship to other ancient megaliths:

> The construction of the enormous roofed stone circles of Stonehenge with architectural features such as tenons and mortice holes cut in the stone shows some relationship to the megalithic stonework of Tiahuanaco and other pre-Inca ruins of South America, not only in some of its construction details but perhaps also in the reasons for its being built—the construction of a gigantic seasonal or astronomical clock with perhaps other features that we have not yet discovered.[5]

It is true that there are remarkable similarities in many of these ancient structures, and one cannot read in depth about such cultures without being impressed by similarities. Sometimes they are in primitive homes —in fact, sometimes there are great similarities to modern constructions, as between the dome-shaped reed huts of the early Sumerians and the "modern" homes of the primitive Todas in South India today.

At other times the general resemblances involve more stately buildings, such as the pyramids in Egypt and Central America alike. As Berlitz points out above, similarities can also be demonstrated between sites as far removed as Stonehenge in England and Tiahuanaco in South America.

Perhaps there were memories of cultural links, or possibly it is simply that intelligent men in different parts of the earth developed their construction styles along similar paths. This latter would be expected, even if the former were also partly true.

Many theories have been advanced about Stonehenge itself. The slaughter stone has been pictured as the place where ruthless priests delighted in cutting the throats of helpless human victims, their own flowing robes changing from white to scarlet red as the blood of their victims flowed.

## The Magic of Merlin?

Another tradition centers around an incident after the Roman army left Britain, when the Saxons slew 460 of the British nobles. The British were eventually able to overthrow the Saxons, and then—so the tradition goes—they raised a monument at Stonehenge to commemorate the activities of those who had been slain. The famous Merlin, the wizard of the king Aurelius Ambrosius, is supposed to have come forward with a plan that was adopted.

It involved stealing the ritual stones from another center that was over the sea in Ireland. This center was supposed to be associated with the dance of the giants. Ancient giants had carried the stones from Africa to set them up in Ireland, and baths with special healing properties against many ailments had been established there. All who came and washed were healed.

According to the legend, King Aurelius dispatched an army to Ireland. The stones associated with the giants' dance were to be stolen and brought to Britain, but the troops were unsuccessful. However, Merlin was able to use his magical powers so that the stones were soon moved down to the seacoast, loaded on a ship, then brought to Stonehenge and established as a great memorial center.

Yet another theory was that of Edmund Bolton in 1864—that in fact Stonehenge was where the English Queen Boadicea had been buried, and the stones were a memorial to commemorate her leadership in a famous revolt against the Romans in the first century A.D.

## A Center of Druid Worship?

Perhaps the most persistent hypothesis is that the ruins are of Druidic origin—this has been one of the most popular theories through the centuries. King James I of England sent an architect named Inigo Jones to report to him on the structure and purpose of Stonehenge. Although Inigo Jones himself concluded that the structures were not Druidic, but probably had originally been a Roman temple, others took up this theory of a Druidic origin of the famous center.

John Aubrey, who discovered the famous "Aubrey Holes," was an eager proponent of this Druidic origin theory. It was Aubrey who discovered that at Avebury, some seventeen miles north of Stonehenge, there was another even larger circular rampart and ditch, again with concentric circles of stones standing inside it. However, it was difficult to investigate, for the village of Avebury was virtually in the center of the inner circles and Avebury had very practical interests in the land itself. In relatively modern times local people had active campaigns to remove the stones—breaking them, burning them, carting them away—because they interfered with their farming and house construction.[6]

This destruction was described by another investigator in the eighteenth century, William Stukeley, who had been both a doctor and an Anglican priest. He became obsessed with Druidism, and believed its teachings could be reconciled with Christianity. He attributes the sites at both Avebury and Stonehenge to Druids, whom he regarded as priests of the Celtic peoples who had once dominated much of Europe.

As far as is known, the Druids had no form of writing, and there are only scraps of information about them from ancient writers of Roman times, such as Julius Caesar, Strabo, Tacitus, and the elder Pliny. There are many legends about them, referring to various pagan customs. According to some of the traditions that have grown up around them, there were also commendable virtues that were not normally associated with ancient priests.

Nevertheless it is more than difficult to accept Stukeley's identification of these people with early Christians. They worshipped many gods who were supposedly incarnations of objects of nature such as mountains, rivers, and even animals. From what we know about them, it seems they did not have temples as such but met in secret places in the woods. They had mystical rites and partook in human sacrifice.

Julius Caesar wrote about their practice of setting human victims on fire, but he suggests there were moral reasons for this practice. According to Caesar, it was the punishment for those who were caught in the act of robbery or other crimes. This reasoning is somewhat different from that associated with most other human sacrifices, but Caesar goes on to say that if they did not find criminals they would sacrifice substitutes—other people who were innocent of any crime. This certainly does not fit Christian teachings.

## The Reemergence of Druidism

Similarities to Christianity there were—such as their opposition to crime. Even in the Druids' refusal to be dominated by the Roman powers, for which they were ruthlessly suppressed, there is a superficial resemblance to Christian noncompliance with Roman worship. However, when eventually Christianity triumphed as the state religion under the Romans, Druidism was no longer a major influence, though some of its customs can still be traced in Western countries. The celebration of Hallowe'en is said to come from the Druids.

A new order of Druids was established in 1781, and many of these cultists took seriously a whole series of literary forgeries which linked the Druids back to the ancient Persians, and through them to the Hebrew patriarchs Noah and Abraham. Even in modern times, on certain days of the year the neo-Druids gather at Stonehenge to undertake their rites. The Chief Bard wears a ceremonial robe of white and gold, and the celebrants wait for the first sign of the rising sun, for at that moment the shadow of the Heel Stone is supposed to fall directly across the altar. Great fires are kindled with torches, and the priests march in procession around the area of Stonehenge, chanting their ritualistic songs.

Despite the popularity of the theory, most archaeologists discount the Druid association with these monuments. Excavators have found coins which date from the times of England's George III back to the Romans, and in some of the earlier levels stone hammers and axes were found, indicating earlier activity by Stone Age men.

## Stonehenge and Sun Worship

The possibility that Stonehenge is associated with the movements of the sun is well described by Sprague and Catherine de Camp as follows:

> In 1901 the Astronomer Royal, Sir Norman Lockyer, measured and calculated the positions of these stones. Lockyer claimed that if one stood on the center of the Altar Stone at dawn on Midsummer Day, one would see the sun rise (if one saw it at all in British weather) almost exactly over the tip of the Heel Stone.
>
> Lockyer, who believed that Stonehenge was built by sun-worshipping Druids, calculated that, at the time Stonehenge was built, the sun rose exactly over the point of the Heel Stone. But the slight periodic increase and decrease in the obliquity of the ecliptic (the angle between the plane of the earth's equator and that of its orbit) had spoiled this alignment. However, knowing the rate of change in the obliquity of the ecliptic (which goes through a complete cycle in 40,000 years) Sir Norman figured back to the date of construction: between −1900 and −1500.[7]

Lockyer's reasoning was actually wrong on a number of counts, but some of his basic conclusions might well be correct. Sprague and Catherine de Camp go on to state that the sun now rises to the left of the Heel Stone on June 21, and in ancient times it rose even farther to the left. They argue that it will not rise directly over the Heel Stone for another 1,000 years. They state that the Heel Stone cannot cast a shadow on the Altar Stone because one of the uprights of the Sarsen Circle stands between the Heel Stone and the altar.

Another reason they give is—as shown above—that some scholars believe that the Altar Stone is not an altar after all, but is simply a fallen upright. They then conclude that, even if the stones were originally aligned as exactly as Lockyer had supposed, this orientation could not now be exactly determined because of the leaning or fall of several of the stones by which that orientation would be measured.

## A Huge Solar Calendar?

The de Camps further state that even if the builders of Stonehenge were not sun worshippers, the fact that the horseshoe faced in the general direction of the rising midsummer sun probably at least indicates that this great structure had some practical purpose associated with keeping track of the time of the year. As these early neolithic farmers had no calendars, this was of great importance to them: "By facing in the direction opposite to that of midsummer sunrise, you face the direction of midwinter sunset and thus have a date from which to count the days to spring planting. The monument may as well have been oriented towards one as towards the other." [8]

Despite the numerous conjectures as to the function of Stonehenge, the fact is that its function is to some extent still an unsolved mystery. From time to time television "specials" give us new constructions, especially as to the associations of the stones with movements of the sun and other heavenly bodies. We are presented with various conjectures and theories as to the religious purpose of the monuments, as when the discovery of the double-axe sign on some of the stones led to the suggestion that there was a link with Minoan civilization in the later building of Stonehenge. Others have suggested a Mycenean Greek or Maltese influence. It all makes fascinating reading, and at times the television specials are very interesting.

## Neither Magic nor Astronauts!

Even bigger monuments than Stonehenge have been constructed with primitive tools, and there is no need to accept Merlin's magic as the way these stones were brought from Wales (not from Ireland, as the legend declared).

In conclusion, it is relevant to notice an interesting point of similarity between Erich Von Daniken and that court magician Merlin who lived in early Britain. With Merlin we read of huge stones being transported from Africa to Ireland . . . of giants dancing . . . of men unable to move them from Ireland to England, then Merlin coming to the rescue. By his magic those massive monoliths could be transported across the sea to England—they were now as light as feathers.

Von Daniken also pictures huge stone giants being juggled over hills and valleys, and he includes the Stonehenge monoliths in this description.[9] How could these and other massive stones be moved? Only by astronaut power of course!

The fact is, our knowledge of ancient technology, which is referred to in our chapters on the pyramids and Easter Island, indicates that men of old could certainly have constructed these monoliths.

We certainly do not need to search for Merlin's

magic. Nor need we go along with Erich Von Daniken as his astronauts come whooshing down from Mars or somewhere else in space. Perhaps we suffer from myopia, but we cannot see those energetic astronauts alighting from their fiery chariots to transmit their extraterrestrial powers to ape-like beings whom they empower to transport huge stones through space, as easily as though they were made of silk.

## CHAPTER 6

# The Marvels and the Myths of the Mayas

The interest in archaeology and ancient things is not limited to so-called cradles of civilization such as Sumer and Egypt, or to great library centers like that at Nineveh. At almost the same time that the famous palaces of Assyria were first being excavated, John Lloyd Stephens was appointed as a diplomatic representative to the United States in Central America.

This was in 1839, and his enthusiasm for ancient civilizations had been developed during travels in Greece some years earlier. Now he set out with Frederick Catherwood, who was just as eager to search for archaeological remains. Catherwood made a great contribution to archaeological knowledge by his accurate drawings of the ruins and other evidences that he and Stephens found. Together they penetrated thickly overgrown jungle and swamps to find ancient civilizations associated with the early Indian inhabitants of Central America.

Stephens eventually found a number of monumental stelae which were more than ten feet high, covered with hieroglyphics and various sculptured figures. He also found a pyramid and a flight of steps that led to a terrace nearly 100 feet high. His interest in the ancient cultures of the Indians of Central America continued until he died in New York in 1852.

## Skeletons in a Well

Another famous explorer in these regions was Edward Herbert Thompson who went to Yucatan as consul for the United States in 1885. He gathered a great amount of material, and took some of the local legends seriously—including one that in ancient times young girls had been sacrificed in the so-called sacred well at Chichén Itzá. The priests were also supposed to have thrown in treasures for the gods. Thompson eventually found skeletons in this seventy-foot-deep well—mainly of teen-aged girls, and a few warriors. He also recovered valuable objects, and all this seemed to suggest that the legends were based on fact.[1]

Erich Von Daniken discusses this well, and tells of Thompson's grisly finds. He then reports that a short distance away there is a second well—"guarded by snakes, poisonous millipedes, and troublesome insects, the hole has the same measurements as the 'real' well." [2] He tells us that the wells "resemble each other most strikingly" and that "possibly they both owe their existence to the impact of meteorites." According to Von Daniken, contemporary scholars speak only of the first well, for the second well "does not fit into their theories." [3]

At first it seems Von Daniken has come up with a "scoop"—information kept secret, hidden from the world because of some mysterious collaboration between parties unnamed. However, there is no mystery. Gordon Whittaker, who specializes in Aztec civilization at Brandeis University, answers Von Daniken's points, stating that "the two wells figure on all the maps of the city" and that they are neither identical nor caused by meteorites crashing to earth. They "were formed when the limestone land-surface collapsed over underground water." Such wells were found all over Yucatan.[4]

Again Von Daniken has taken a series of interesting facts and added a sensational note that lends color to what he is saying.

## The Mayan Calendar

He tells us many other amazing things about these Mayas:

They left behind not only a fabulous calendar but also incredible calculations. They knew the Venusian year of 584 days and estimated the duration of the terrestrial year at 365.2420 days. (The exact calculation today: 365.2422!) The Mayas left behind them calculations to last for 64,000,000 years. Later inscriptions dealt in units which probably approach 400,000,000 years. The famous Venusian formula could quite plausibly have been calculated by an electronic brain. At any rate, it is difficult to believe that it originated from a jungle people.[5]

He also tells us it was not because they needed them that the Mayas built pyramids and temples, but because their calendar decreed that a fixed number of steps of a building were to be completed every fifty-two years. Thus he sees every stone as having a relationship to the calendar, and every completed building conforming exactly to specific requirements of astronomy. These were religious requirements, for, according to Von Daniken, "At some point in a very early period the Mayas' ancestors were paid a visit by the 'gods' (in whom I suspect space travelers)." [6] He tells us that among the Mayas there were strictly guarded sacred traditions that related to astronomy, mathematics, and the calendar.

The priests supposedly guarded this knowledge because the "gods" had promised that one day they would return, and so these priests created "a grandiose new religion, the religion of Kukulkán, the Feathered Serpent." [7] That return would be when the vast building complex was completed according to the laws set by this calendar cycle. Von Daniken then tells us that the promised time arrived but the gods did not return. The Mayas' work had ended, and soon their civilization collapsed. They migrated to the north where they established a new kingdom with more cities, temples, and pyramids, all constructed according to further dates that also were set by their calendar.[8]

## Astronauts Not Needed!

Gordon Whittaker has a further relevant comment at this point. He says that Von Daniken "emphasizes that all Maya structures were built according to the dictates of the Maya calendar, and to illustrate his claim he states that the Toltec pyramid at Chichén Itzá known today as El Castillo—the Castle—has the same number of steps up it as there are days in the year. It takes little more than patience to work out how many days there are in a year—you note where the sun sets on a certain day and count how many days it takes to reappear at that spot. Astronauts are not needed for that."[9]

Undoubtedly the Mayan calendar was remarkable, as we shall see, but once again we cannot go along with Von Daniken. Actually it is not necessary to answer his theory, for he himself acknowledges that it is no more than a theory. He states, "I should like to introduce a new note into the concert of opinions, a theory that is not proved any more than the other interpretations are."[10] However, he does not present it as though it is merely an unproven hypothesis, for, in his own words, "Regardless of the probability of the other explanations, I venture to make my contribution boldly and with conviction."[11]

He even gives us a date of 3111 B.C. for the beginning date for the Mayan calendar, and suggests that "if we accept this date as proved, then there was only a gap of a few hundred years between it and the beginning of the Egyptian culture."[12] What is proved? The fact is, no common starting point has been found to relate this calendar to other calendars. This is simply another point at which the hypotheses of Von Daniken are pure Von Danikenisms.

Putting his theories to one side, what are the facts? These people did not develop their writing forms beyond a relatively simple stage of hieroglyphics, but this seems to have been adequate for their needs. One major purpose of writing was to record months, days, and other information especially important in relation to their calendar. Sometimes their hieroglyphics (known as glyphs) were carved on stone, but at other times they were painted on ceramics or carved on bone. Their script has not been deciphered, though research continues, and some of the glyphs relating to numbers can now be read.

It is true that their calendar has astonished archaeologists, as have many of the other accomplishments of these Central American people. Their calendar shows that they had a remarkably accurate knowledge of astronomy, and they were able to make exact observations and calculations relating to the movements of the sun, the moon, and many of the planets and stars. They constructed observatories in which they measured and recorded data relating to astronomical events. They could even predict eclipses accurately.

## The Mayas' Use of Mathematics

Their achievements in mathematics were also remarkable. This ability was carried over into their astronomical calculations, for they were able to know the margin of error necessary to bring their calendar back into line from time to time.

Archaeologists have been able to work out details of the Mayan system of counting time. The calendar was based on the movements of the sun, but instead of our twelve months it actually had eighteen, with twenty days each, and then one month with only five days, thus totaling 365 days. Each month had its own name, and each of the twenty days was known by a number and by a name on a written glyph as well.

The system was quite complex, but it did not end there. Yet another division was made of the solar year whereby there were twenty-eight groups consisting of thirteen days each, and again a day was added at the end, making 365 days for the year. It was recognized that a complete cycle of years took place every fifty-two years. The system had other intricate details, with both mystical and practical significance, and its precision was quite remarkable.

These Mayan people are yet another example of an ancient race who had a surprisingly modern knowledge of the movements of the sun, the moon, and the stars. Their buildings and their numerous stelae (memorial pillars) had many hieroglyphics on them, and these reliefs were also linked to their calendar as religious and secular records were brought together.

On the surface it would seem to be a relatively easy thing to find a point of synchronization between the Mayan calendar and our own, but as yet no common dating point has been identified. Thus a comparative chronology can be worked out only in broad outline.

Von Daniken also refers to this remarkable mathematical knowledge of the Mayas and other ancient peoples. He makes much of supposedly amazing numbers—numbers with fifteen digits that could not be registered by any computer. Dr. Colin Gauld tells us that this argument is utter nonsense—that they can be registered by computers. He says:

> The list of figures . . . again looks impressive but how it is supposed to give any idea of the accuracy of the Mayan Calendar is difficult to see. From this list two conclusions can be drawn. The first is that the Mayas could multiply 20 by 18 by 20 by 20 by 20 by 20 by 20 by 20 and come up with the correct answer of $23,040,000,000$. (What the small subscripts 2 and 1 in the answer are sup-

posed to mean is not explained.) The second is that if this is a calendar then one "tun" appears to be the same as a year and 360 days is not very accurate at all. These figures seem at odds with the figures . . . which are also related to the Mayan Calendar. How are we to conclude anything about its accuracy from the data given? [13]

## The History of Peoples in Central and South America

Erich Von Daniken talks at some length about the Mayan and other civilizations of Central and South America, and it is relevant to look briefly at the history of these various peoples.

Before the Mayas there had been an earlier civilization in this Mexican area—the Olmec peoples who established their religious centers around Tabasco and Vera Cruz. They accomplished amazing things with only stone tools—including a famous nine-foot-tall sculptured head in stone, from San Lorenzo.

At this point it is relevant to refer to yet another Von Danikenism. He says that no bridge could stand the weight of these great colossii of the Olmecs of Mexico, and that they will therefore never be on show in a museum. However, in *Some Trust in Chariots,* Gordon Whittaker points out that some of these giant heads are actually found in museums. He further states that "one was recently transported thousands of miles to the Metropolitan Museum of Art in New York for a special exhibition." [14] Another is on display in Houston, Texas.

Actually many of the sculptures have been transported across country, to such places as Villa-herruosa in Mexico. That particular site is about seventy-five miles from where the colossii were originally constructed.

## *The Mayas in History*

Mayan history is believed to have extended from about 150 A.D. to 1450 A.D., with the dates divided up as follows—about 150 to 600 A.D. the Old Empire; about 600 to 1000 A.D. the migration to Yucatán; about 1000 A.D. to 1450 A.D. the New Empire. Some scholars suggest an earlier beginning date, approximately the first century B.C.

These people lived on the plateaus of Central America about the same time that the Romans controlled the "Western World." They left behind traces of temples, cities, and palaces constructed in stone. Their high cultural level was maintained until not long before Columbus rediscovered the American continent.

The original Mayan settlements were in southern and eastern Mexico, and these people were successful agriculturists. Permanent communities were developed with relatively large villages. It is evident from their artefacts and potsherds, as well as their everyday cups, dishes, weapons of war, and other implements, that they were capable craftsmen. They utilized metals and precious stones, and some of their gold and jade jewelry was beautiful by any standards.

It is not known why they deserted those areas now known as Mexico, though various researchers have conjectured epidemics, sudden invasions, or natural calamities. We do not know the answer. However, we do know that when they migrated to the Yucatán Peninsula somewhere before 1000 A.D., once again they built massively in stone and achieved a further magnificent culture.

It seems that the migration to Yucatán was preceded by a series of wars between rival cities, leading to economic and political chaos, and their magnificent civilization declined. As with the ancient sites of the classical world, the remnants of the civilization were plundered, and great quantities of stone and building materials were carried off for the construction of other buildings and of roads.

The houses in the villages and towns were not made of stone, but were simpler structures of mud brick and thatch. It was the public buildings in which stone was utilized, buildings that were clearly meant to withstand the ravages of time. These buildings were impressive indeed—sometimes the stones weighed up to forty tons. They had to be transported overland, then raised into their positions in pyramids and other massive structures. Many lime kilns for cement have been found. They also burnt limestone to make the plaster with which they coated the outside facings of their buildings.

Their massive structures were mainly associated with either religion or government, and their temples were usually in the form of a pyramid. Strictly they were not true pyramids, for they were a series of terraces with flat tops, instead of a point, as with most of the Egyptian pyramids. The flat top often served as a base for an altar, and it could be reached by steps from the ground.

The chief god of the Mayas was Kukulcán, usually shown as a serpent covered with feathers. His image is on many of the Mayan pyramids.

## The Toltecs Build Their Pyramids

Another people who flourished in Mexico from about 500 A.D. to 1100 A.D. were the Toltecs, though scholars debate the dates of these and other Latin-American cultures. It seems that the Toltecs first appeared in the Valley of Mexico about 500 A.D., and their empire was at its height about 1000 A.D. Like the Mayas, they migrated to Yucatán somewhere about 1000 to 1100 A.D. One of their most famous ancient cities was Teotihuacán, located not very far north of modern Mexico City.

Tollan and Cholula are two more of their ancient cities that have been studied by archaeologists.

The Toltecs also built an elaborate system of pyramids and temples, and some of their ruins are still to be seen stretching over several miles near Teotihuacán. Two great pyramids at this center were of special importance, one being erected to the sun and the other to the moon. They are still very well preserved and demonstrate the remarkable engineering ability of these people.

There has been controversy as to whether they were built by the Aztecs or the Toltecs, but they appear to antedate the Aztecs' empire, and this did not appear in the Valley of Mexico until about 1300 A.D. The Toltecs also built a number of pyramid temples which they dedicated to their serpent god Quetzalcoatl. One of these pyramids consists of eight structures, one on top of another, and archaeologists usually report that these successive structures are separated by a time span of fifty-two years each.

There are strong cultural similarities to the Mayas with whom the Toltecs were contemporary, though the Mayas appear to have outlived them in history.

## The Aztecs' Highly Organized Empire

The Aztecs were also important contributors to the culture of this Central American area. It is usually agreed that they migrated into Mexico from the north about 1300 A.D., and built their capital city of Tenoch-titlán, the same site as the present Mexico City.

These people were highly skilled as engineers and built bridges and dikes as well as their pyramid-type temples. They also had a magnificent culture, and when Cortez and his Spanish invaders conquered them in 1519 they carried off vast quantities of beautiful treasures.

Like some of their neighbors, the Aztecs worshipped

the feathered serpent god, and they also called him Quetzalcoatl. At times they practiced human sacrifice, though not to the same extent as some of their neighbors. They were also somewhat more sophisticated than the peoples around them, in that they had a greater interest in building great monuments for their gods.

Like the Maya people, the Aztecs had an accurate calendar, and this was cut on to a large circular stone about twelve feet in diameter and three feet thick. Once again Von Daniken manages to confuse us, for he refers to the Aztec Calendar as a Maya calendar. Gordon Whittaker points out:

> Among the photographs in *Return to the Stars* there is one of the Aztec calendar stone, here labelled as a round Maya calendar, although the two civilizations are quite distinct and there is no way the calendar stone can be considered Maya. Nor are telescopes necessary items for constructing a calendar, although Von Daniken obviously thinks otherwise.[15]

In the main, the Aztecs borrowed from the Mayas and the Toltecs—so much so that it seems they had little native originality. Nevertheless they utilized the best aspects of cultures around them and developed a very well-organized empire. In 1519 that empire was cut to shreds by the Spanish invaders under Cortez, and the Aztec people themselves were slaughtered mercilessly.

## The Incas of Peru

Farther south, in the area we now know as Peru, the Inca people founded an empire, establishing their capital at Cuzco about 1000 A.D. Actually the word "Inca" means ruler, and was the title of the emperor. The people looked on their emperor as a god-man and they were his subjects. Eventually all the people ruled by him became known as Incas.

The Inca had a whole series of officials well placed throughout his empire, and that empire was highly organized, both politically and religiously. The workforce was directed in no uncertain terms, with the Inca able to decide who would be enlisted in the army and those who would be employed in mines. Farmers had to pay tribute, both for the upkeep of the temples and for the administration of the government.

Over a period of 400 years the empire expanded considerably in all directions, and extensive building operations established these people as remarkably developed in culture. They connected their more important towns with stone-paved roads, and some of them can still be used. They were expert stone-cutters, and the precision with which the stones in their buildings were joined is still a cause of great wonder.

We have seen that to the north the people of Central America built temple pyramids, with some similarity to those constructed in early Egypt. However, the Inca people did not build pyramids but constructed their temples in rectangular shapes.

They would also terrace the whole of a mountainside, first having to clear all the jungle area. Some of their buildings were quite remarkable, including circular constructions. High up in the mountains they built their beautiful granite houses, with their stonework fitting meticulously.

Professor Hiram Bingham of Yale University rediscovered some of these magnificent structures in 1911, and went back the following year with a larger expedition, under the auspices of his university and the National Geographic Society. The expedition found roads, houses, and even a tunnel through a cliff. In 1914 and 1915 Bingham led further expeditions to explore these fantastic evidences of a past glory. The ruins that he investigated especially were known locally as "Machu Picchu."

## Hilltop Fortresses and Temples

Machu Picchu was a *pucara*—a hilltop fortress which could be used by the local people in case of attack. This city consisted of narrow streets, with many houses crowded together, and no less than 100 different stairways hewn out of the rock. Some of them had as many as 150 steps, and at times ten steps would be cut from one huge boulder.

A huge fortress at Sacsahuaman is believed to have been the *pucara* for the old Inca capital of Cuzco— Sacsahuaman was surrounded by huge walls, sometimes as high as sixty feet, and it has been estimated that some of its stones weighed up to 200 tons.

The Incas erected great stone temples which at times were 300 feet in length. One of the best known was the Temple of the Sun at Cuzco, and both its inside and outside walls were covered with gold, for gold was supposed to represent the sun's brightness.

The Incas were finally conquered by the Spaniards under Pizarro in 1533: they were plundered, and their civilization was destroyed. From that time on, their culture declined and eventually disappeared, as had the Olmecs, the Mayas, the Toltecs, and the Aztecs before them.

The Incas left fantastic evidence of advanced culture, but unfortunately they did not leave behind written records. The reconstruction of their civilization must come from archaeological research, and many problems remain unanswered.

## The Chariots Still Crash—in Peru

In our next chapter we deal with the lines on the Nazca Plain, much of the information coming from an interview with the Reverend Donald Bond who lives at Nazca. At that time I asked him a number of other questions. The first was about the huge stone at Sacsahuaman in Peru, to which Erich Von Daniken had referred. Von Daniken claims that there was a huge stone block there, with an estimated weight of 20,000 tons. He goes on to tell of a single stone block that is the size of a four-story house. It is supposedly impeccably dressed in the most craftsmanlike way, and has steps and ramps. That is not all: he tells us that the stone is upside down.[16] In *Crash Go the Chariots* we discussed this stone megalith, and we suggested—in answer to Von Daniken's question: "What power overturned it? What titanic forces were at work here?"—that an earthquake could have been responsible. There is no great problem about the steps that run down the side of the great stone, for these are similar to the steps in the terraced mountainsides for which the Incas have become famous. In *Crash Go the Chariots* we submitted evidence that some stone pillars *had* been restored upside down.

However, when this matter was put to Mr. Bond, he pointed out that Von Daniken had cleverly covered himself by saying that this huge stone is not at the Sacsahuaman that is known by the general public. It is supposedly some secret Sacsahuaman, half a mile away from the well-known Inca fortress.

Mr. Bond has been a missionary in Peru for over fifteen years, and he stated that he had never heard of this secret Sacsahuaman. He is familiar with Sacsahuaman, but the heaviest stone there is calculated to weigh 200 tons, and the fact is that *this* stone is pointed out as being the heaviest of all of those used by the Incas. It is well known locally. As Mr. Bond said, "You can stand a man beside it as I have done and take a picture of it. The stone would be about twelve feet in height—twice the height of a reasonably tall man."

## Was It 200 Tons or 20,000 Tons?

He reiterated that this is pointed out as being the

heaviest stone ever used by the Incas, and that it is in a place with the same name as this mysterious secret place to which Erich Von Daniken refers. He wondered if perhaps Von Daniken had added a few zeroes, making a stone of 200 tons into one that is 20,000 tons.

Mr. Bond further stated, "The quarry from which these stones were taken has been found—it is about three or four miles from the fort at Sacsahuaman. It is believed that the stones were moved on rollers—wooden poles. The Incas had vast manpower resources, for the rulers had at their disposal all the men throughout their whole empire. These people were highly disciplined, and there would have been many thousands of men available to move any of those stones. It is not an impossibility at all, as Von Daniken implies. They certainly did not need space machines or anything like that to move them. It seems they were rolled along on wooden rollers, and that is a relatively easy process."

The date given for these constructions in Peru is about 1000 A.D. If we were to accept Von Daniken's hypothesis of visitors from space helping in the building, we would need a series of such visits. It is clearly a quite different time period from the building of the pyramids in Egypt and other structures for which Von Daniken also suggests the help of visiting astronauts. The time difference is considerably more than 3,000 years.

My next question to Mr. Bond was about the records left behind by the Inca people, to which he replied: "The Incas did not leave any written records, and this is one of the notable exceptions to their high civilization. Von Daniken would not agree with me at this point, for he tells us about a supposed book in South America 'that contained all the wisdom of antiquity'; Von Daniken goes on to say that 'it is reputed to have been destroyed by the sixty-third Inca ruler, Pachacuti IV.' [17]

"I have never heard of Pachacuti IV, and I assure you that I have read all I have been able to find about these Inca people. I could not even suggest what language this supposed book would have been written in. It certainly could not have been written in Quechua, the language of the Incas, because they had no writing. I have worked with the Quechua people for a short time, though most of my work in Peru has been with other people, over on the Amazon River."

## Recording on Quipas

"These Inca people had what were called *quipas,* and quite a number of them are still in existence—they were different colored strings with knots on them. Von Daniken does not mention the *quipas,* but leads us to believe that these Inca people had writing. I have read all the authorities that I could, such as William Prescott and Von Hagan, and I have studied under Quechua instructors from San Marcos University in Lima— Quechua was the language of the Inca Empire, and the Incas had no writing.

"It is important to understand that the Inca Empire was very highly socialized, and there were granaries and storehouses scattered at strategic points throughout the empire. There were inventories of all the food and fabrics, and everything else that was stored at these strategic centers. They even had records on the *quipas* as to how many able-bodied men were in each of the towns—they knew the numbers that could be called on throughout the empire for road-building or other projects. They also recorded various things about the days of the years.

"However, one serious disadvantage of the *quipa* was that only the man who made it could read it—you could not take someone else's *quipa* and read what he was saying. That is the reason why *quipas* cannot be read today."

Pressed as to the fact that Von Daniken implied that all sorts of written messages were associated with the records of these ancient people, Reverend Bond insisted, "No writing has ever been found, and I have read all that I could lay my hands on as to their history. I have seen a very great number of the Inca ruins, including their capital city. There are no inscriptions of any kind on any of the stones, or on any of the walls. There are many drawings, but no inscriptions. There is absolutely no writing of any kind found on the walls, on their pottery, or on anything else that I have ever seen. This is not only my personal belief, for my own experience is paralleled by what the authorities insist on at this point. Even the priests who went in with the Spanish conquerors reported that they found no writings."

## Weaving . . . Platinum . . . Jade

Mr. Bond had a number of other relevant comments, and what follows to the end of this chapter is my editing of his answers to my questions.

"Von Daniken states that the Incas had no weaving, and the implication is that they were taught it by the astronauts. Anybody who knows anything at all about the history of the Incas will tell you they were famous for their weaving—they utilized fine cotton cloths, and these were beautifully colored with inks and dyes. In fact, one of the ways by which the different cultures in these areas have been distinguished is by their cloth. A culture known as 'Paraces' had one sort of cotton cloth, while the people in the Nazca culture had another type. Although these two regions are near each other, the people had distinctive weaving patterns at different periods of time as their cultures developed separately. It is recognized that one of the ways to tell the change from one age to another is by the type of weaving, and by the figures they used in their weaving.

"This art was known long ago among the early Incas.

Their very fine weaving was recognized as being exceptionally good—experts say it is some of the best ever found in the world. Von Daniken is clearly in error at this point.

"While we are talking about his errors, Von Daniken also makes much about ornaments of smelted platinum being found on the Peruvian Plateau. However, there is a lot of platinum in the Andes Mountains: it is actually mined there today—I believe it is one of the most important areas in the world for the mining of platinum. The explanation of the smelting of platinum is no problem, for the Incas melted gold and silver and made beautiful ornaments right through their history. Von Daniken makes a special point of telling us that 'ornaments of smelted platinum were found on the Peruvian Plateau . . . This strange medley of "impossibilities" should make us curious and uneasy.' [18]

"They are not 'impossibilities' at all, but unfortunately as many people read this sort of statement they would tend to think, 'Well, there must have been astronauts—they brought their metals with them.' However, the metals that have been found and are supposedly associated with these astronauts, are invariably found in the local area.

"Von Daniken made a similar point about Guatemala —that it was a miracle that jade was found in Guatemala because jade comes from China. [19] The fact is, jade is relatively common in the river beds of Central and South America."

## Those Astronauts in Their Rockets

One of Von Daniken's most publicized pictures is in the center of *Chariots of the Gods?*, and his caption states, "This drawing was made in the temple at Copán. Could primitive imagination have produced anything so remarkably similar to a modern astronaut in his rocket? The strange markings at the foot of the drawing can only be an indication of the flames and gases coming from the propulsion unit."

Von Daniken has a similar description in the body of *Chariots of the Gods?*, this time about a stone relief "that very probably represents the god Kukumatz (in Yucatán, Kukulkán)—found in the old kingdom of Palenque." Von Daniken tells us that "a genuinely unprejudiced look at this picture would make even the most die-hard skeptic stop and think." [20]

He goes on to describe this god-man who supposedly sits with the upper part of his body bent forward like a racing motorcyclist, while he manipulates a number of indefinable controls. Von Daniken talks about indentations and tubes and says there was something like an antennae on top. He then tells us that this being is clearly depicted as a space traveler. [21]

This picture has caused great interest around the world, and a surprising number of people have suggested that at least this one picture should be taken seriously. Could it possibly depict an astronaut who visited Earth long ago?

In view of Von Daniken's suggestion that the second "astronaut" figure represented one of the gods of these people, it was relevant to ask Mr. Bond for his interpretation of the whole picture, and it was very interesting:

"Von Daniken is talking about one of the Maya gods, whereas in Peru where I live and work the people were Incas. However, there were similarities in worship between the Mayas, the Aztecs, and the Incas. The people carried their emperors round in chairs, and the picture Von Daniken shows is of a king or a god on his throne. There are very similar pictures with the Incas.

"We quoted Von Daniken as stating that 'a genuinely unprejudiced look at this picture would make even the most die-hard skeptic stop and think,' [22] but actually one would need a very good imagination to make the interpretation that Von Daniken does. This man is simply sitting on a throne, and he appears to be looking toward the heavens, obviously relaxing. He has bare feet, and he would hardly go shooting off into space without protection for his feet! It is not at all unusual to see bare feet in a picture such as this, for many of the people in these parts of the world still wear bare feet most of the time.

"This man is sitting sideways, with his feet resting on one of the arms, and sometimes the rulers would ride like this for many miles. They would often change their position, for a person being carried by teams of men over long distances would hardly sit as a king would sit when facing his audience. He would relax, change his position, and put his feet up—and that is what this picture shows. He could hardly sit in the same position for twelve hours or more! As a matter of fact, it seems that this man has a cushion behind his head and he might even be sleeping.

"The ruler or a member of the Royal Family might be carried all day in a chair such as this by relays of men—they did the work of animals in carrying such a throne over long distances, for the Mayas did not use the types of animals that could have drawn a vehicle— they did not have horses, donkeys, or bullocks.

"These rulers had very elaborate thrones and chairs on which they were carried all over their kingdom, and it would have been just this type of conveyance."

## Flames and Gases?

"Von Daniken talks about strange markings at the foot of the drawings, and suggests that these can only be an indication of flames and gases that are shooting up from the unit, but when you look at it you find it is nothing but the legs of the throne. This could not possibly be a rocket—you can easily trace the way the arms turn in on the throne, and you can see a backrest at the top. You can see the legs of the throne, and there is a back piece that goes up behind the man's head.

"There are two serpents sticking up near the man's head—serpents were common in their religious drawings and rites, for it was an important god in animistic worship. Notice that the serpents are outside the so-called space chariot—we wonder why a space traveler would want to take a couple of serpents with him!

"It is relevant also to point out that in other places Von Daniken refers to space guns and communications equipment associated with these 'spacemen.' There is no mystery about those things—there are many of them in various history books, and the so-called helmets and antennae are common things like masks, hairdresses, and even bows and arrows."

## Fasten Seat Belts!

Clearly one of Von Daniken's leading witnesses— that seated astronaut—is not so convincing after all. The spaceman is nothing more than a mere mortal, and his space journey was really rather boring, bumping along at the fantastic speed of five miles an hour or thereabouts, according to the athletic prowess of the relays of slaves who were "privileged" to carry his space vehicle over the Mayan countryside.

The chariots certainly keep crashing, but before we leave this fascinating continent we must consider one more subject in some detail. We refer to those mysterious lines on the Nazca Plain in Peru. Our good friend the Reverend Donald Bond lives there, and he has an interesting story to tell. So, fasten seat belts as we zoom in on that place which to Erich Von Daniken was reminiscent of an aircraft parking area in a modern airport.

# The Man from Nazca

I have never been to Nazca in Peru, but I will not soon forget an indirect contact I had with that famous old city.

I was guest speaker for a special series at the Calvary Baptist Church in Binghamton, New York. I arrived there on a Saturday evening, and enjoyed visiting with Pastor and Mrs. Jack Beukema. After some time, I arranged to be at the church at ten thirty the next morning, then went off to the motel where I was to stay for the next few days.

It had been a hectic week. I had jetted across the world from Melbourne, Australia, had spent some time in California on an educational project with which I am deeply involved, and then had a series of late night and early morning committee meetings in Schenectady, New York, before coming on to Binghamton.

By the time I got back to the motel I was exceedingly tired, but foolishly worked at my typewriter until about 2:30 A.M. Then I went to bed, having no concern about the heavy curtains being drawn, for I knew from experience—or did I?—that I would be well and truly awake six or seven hours later. I would be in plenty of time for the next day's commitments, even though I had gone to bed so late.

I was awakened by the telephone ringing, and when I answered it, my friend Pastor Jack Beukema asked, "Have you forgotten all about us?"

"What do you mean—what's the time?" I asked.

"It's eleven o'clock," he told me. "We're just about to start the service."

"I'm terribly sorry," I said, "I didn't wake until I

heard the telephone, but I'll be there by eleven thirty. I suppose you have preliminaries for that long?"

"It happens we have a member of our own church here—he's a missionary in Peru, and he'll take a brief part in the service. Don't worry—so long as you're here by eleven thirty!"

I was there by 11:29 A.M., just as the missionary from Peru was completing his part in the service. Nobody minded the late arrival of the man from "down under" in Australia, for they had heard another man from almost as far down under anyway!

## "I Live in Nazca!"

That missionary was the Reverend Donald Bond, and later I thanked him for the way he had helped me out. Then he said a significant thing.

"By the way, I live in Nazca—you wrote about it in your book *Crash Go the Chariots*."

Needless to say, I arranged an interview with Mr. Bond, and I taped it. A great deal of the information that follows is based on that interview.

Mr. Bond has been a missionary in Peru for seventeen years, much of the time navigating the rivers, but at present he lives in the city of Nazca. He returned there about one week after I talked to him.

My first question concerning the Nazca Plain related to the lines that Erich Von Daniken had suggested might be part of an airfield. I was not surprised that Mr. Bond had other ideas, for he said, "It is foolishness to suggest that those lines on the Nazca Plain have been an airfield. Anyone who has been there would know that this is absolutely impossible. Von Daniken might have seen them from the air, as I gather from his book, but from the ground anyone can see that this theory is impossible—it is not even a hypothesis that could be taken seriously. It is absurd. It is true that these lines are something of a mystery: the authorities and scientists who have studied them do not understand their exact purpose, but there are many other theories much more sensible than this one by Von Daniken.

"I am convinced that anybody who speaks sincerely about the Nazca lines as roads could not have actually been there on the ground itself—it would be impossible to accept such a theory if you have been there on the ground. Von Daniken states in his book: 'Seen from the air, the clear-cut impression that the thirty-seven-mile-long plain of Nazca made on me was that of an airfield.' [1]

"It stands to reason that if this *was* an airfield, or a space center, there would also be the remains of launching pads and various buildings. There is no such evidence of course—even though the extremely dry climate would ensure their preservation."

## What Is So Far-Fetched?

"Von Daniken has seen these lines only from the air—from an airplane. Even then it is hard to accept that he really believed that such little lines could be landing strips for spacecraft or even airplanes. They obviously have nothing to do with an airport, yet Von Daniken asks, 'What is so far-fetched about the idea?' His question is easily answered, for who would build a road four inches wide? What purpose could such a line have as a road, unless someone intended playing with toy cars on it?

"The lines are certainly not wide enough to mark out the landing field of an airport, for, as I have said, most of them would be about four to six inches in width, though some that go for short distances are wider—up to about three feet wide. I have also seen two others that would be perhaps 100 feet wide, but those are in a cleared area that would be only about 200 or 300 feet in length. No one knows what they are.

"I have also seen two different lines that are about fifty feet across. They have cleared away the stones and the dirt and piled the stones up along the side. Then they packed down the dirt on the plain itself, and they apparently mixed some type of a powder in with the dirt. These particular lines are out in the middle of a field: they run for perhaps 200 or 300 feet in length, and then they end. They are more like half of a soccer field than roads, and this area could not be for people to land on because of the high mounds of stones and dirt at the sides."

## That Supposed Parking Area

"The surface of the ground is desert—only about half an inch of rain falls each year. This is the driest desert in the world, according to the encyclopedias. The Nazca lines are out in the desert, and there are blackish brown rocks all over the area, including where the lines are.

"These stones are not big enough to stop cars driving across—they are just small stones: the largest would be the size of a man's fist. In *Chariots of the Gods?* there is a picture of a supposed parking area at an airport, and you can see some of these stones and, calculating from their size, Von Daniken's 'parking area' would be about three or four feet across. I am not referring to just one line, but the whole area of double lines which make up his 'parking area.' The Incas cleaned off the dark-colored rocks from the desert surface, and that is part of the reason why the lines show up so well—they stood out against the sand.

"As I have said, they are quite shallow, often only a half inch to an inch in depth. They certainly would not be suitable for landing a spacecraft on! These shallow little indentations of about half an inch appear to have been made by impacting the ground in some way. There is a crumbly, plasterlike little cap in there usually—it seems they impacted the lines with some sort of powder so that the wind would not move the sand.

"There are heavy winds from time to time—we have a lot of what are called 'witches' winds—these are small whirlwinds. However, the soil is a heavy sand, and as I said, it has a lot of blackish rock in it. The wind simply does not do any damage to the lines. They do not appear to have been damaged at all by erosion or weather. The tracks of cars, trucks, people, and even animals simply stay there indefinitely, this being true of the whole desert area. One reason is that there is virtually no rain to wash them away."

## Inca and Maya Roads

"Von Daniken says it is a preposterous idea to suggest that these lines are Inca roads. I also think it is a preposterous suggestion, but for different reasons from his. Properly formed Inca roads run all through the Andes, but these lines have nothing to do with those roads—they are obviously very different, as anyone seeing them from the ground must immediately concede.

"Inca roads run all through the Andes Mountains, and this was one of the factors that gave cohesion to the Inca Empire. Also, armies could move rapidly over them, and in this there is a similarity to the ancient Roman Empire. The Inca roads were usually about three meters in width and they ran the whole length of their empire which extended over 1,000 miles. These roads can also be seen in Ecuador, Bolivia, and Chile. Some are still in use today, and outstanding books have been written about them.

"The Incas were not the only ones to build such roads. In your book *Crash Go the Chariots* you quote J. Eric S. Thompson, the well-known archaeologist who wrote at length about the Mayas, and he describes a number of Mayan roads. He pointed out that although the

Mayas were inferior to the Incas in road-building, the Mayas also had fantastic straight roads. One went from Coba to Yaxuna, a distance of sixty-two miles, and it ran absolutely straight for many miles—two sections run for twenty and twenty-two miles, respectively. The theory is that these roads were constructed in straight lines by taking sightings from particular stars at night. In the daytime the workers would continue their road-building for the ascertained distance, and when it was necessary they would take another sighting. The straightness of the Nazca lines could be explained by this same process.

"Coming back to the Incas, they carefully studied the heavens and astronomy in general. No doubt they would have used their knowledge in practical ways such as road-building, for they made use of the heavenly bodies in every way possible. The Incas worshipped the sun as their main god, and they worshipped the moon as the sun's wife, and also the stars. The Inca was the ruler over the Inca Empire, and he was supposed to be a direct descendant of the sun."

## The Views of Maria Reiche

"Sometimes it is claimed that these Inca lines were astronomical and calendrical in nature, and I believe this theory is correct. There is a lady scientist, Maria Reiche, who has been in Nazca for over twenty years. She has studied these lines more than anyone else, and she believes that this is the explanation.

"Maria Reiche believes that geometric principles were utilized in the construction of these huge figures in the desert: pivot rocks were used, together with long cords. In *Time* magazine of March 30, 1974, she showed how this was apparently undertaken. Alongside some of the huge figures there are miniatures of the same 'drawings,' in plots six feet square. These were drawn out on a much larger scale by using cords, thus producing the Nazca Plain etchings. She points out that some of these pivoted stones and markings are still in position—they had been used for centering the arcs and circles that are an integral part of a number of the designs.

"Obviously the Incas knew the whole plan from one end to the other before they started, and now we know they did it by using cords, pivot points, and straightforward geometric considerations. This is a relatively simple thing to do. Once the lines of the model are there, you simply take your cord and trace it out, and enlarge it on the desert's surface.

"I have seen some of these level plots—they are about six or eight feet in length and width. Each plot was first cleared of all stones and everything else. Maria Reiche says that on some of the plots you can still see small editions of the larger etchings, but I have not seen these. Perhaps I should stress that there are thousands of these lines, and I have not studied them extensively as Maria Reiche has done. She would know many secrets that are not readily accessible to the more or less casual visitor.

"The Incas were able to coordinate the angles and curves that were necessary as they drew these figures of birds, animals, the constellations and so on. Some of the etchings are very large—for instance, I believe one bird is something like 300 feet in length. You cannot see from one end to the other of some figures, for small hills and other natural features intrude. Sometimes the lines run right over the hill, and it is difficult to see how they could have been drawn without some plan such as Maria Reiche suggests."

## No Prehistoric Airfield in the Andes

"Actually these lines extend over three separate areas, divided by valleys. Quite a deep valley runs down between the separate areas where the lines are found. These lines actually go up and down a number of steep ravines, and there could be no thought of an aircraft—ancient or modern—landing in much of this area. Clearly this is not a continuous air strip!

"It is also a misrepresentation to say the lines are thirty-seven miles long and one mile wide, as though it is a landing strip. That is not the way it is at all. The lines run diagonally, and across, and in all different directions throughout that whole area. None of the lines covers the full length of the area. The fact is, there are no such things as thirty-seven-mile-long Nazca lines.

"Maria Reiche says that the lines extend for thirty miles, and the area certainly is more than a mile wide as Von Daniken claims. I have been back into these lines at least three miles, and I did not get to the end of them. The total plain is probably six or eight miles across, extending to the foothills of the mountains.

"That touches on another minor point, relating to a question on the front cover of *Chariots of the Gods?*— 'Is there evidence of a prehistoric airfield in the Andes?' Strictly speaking, these lines are not in the Andes but are on the coastal plain that leads across to the foothills of the Andes. They are right on the Pan-American Highway, and that highway does not go into the Andes themselves."

## Camping on the Nazca Lines

"Maria Reiche constantly protests that this Pan-American Highway cuts straight through the middle of the lines and has destroyed many of them. She has written at least two books about the Nazca lines, but has withdrawn these from sale. I understand this was done partly to prevent publicity that could be harmful to the future preservation of the lines. She does not like publicity about the lines at all, because there is absolutely no control over the people who are beginning to show up in larger numbers. There are often several cars a day, with people pulling off the highway, camping right on the lines, and driving all over them. These people are ruining the lines, and this is a matter of very great concern to Maria Reiche.

"About ten years ago the Peruvian Army even carried out maneuvers there and drove tanks and trucks over the top of the lines. The tracks of the tanks are still plainly visible. They are far more like roads than the Nazca lines are.

"This touches on another thing that should be said about the pictures in the middle of Von Daniken's book *Chariots of the Gods?* He shows a great mass of these lines, but many of those he shows are obviously car tracks—in fact, in some areas the car tracks have practically obliterated the original lines.

"Another point is that Von Daniken has a plan showing a whole lot of so-called roads, and he says that the archaeologists say they are Inca roads. As we have seen, no archaeologist would say they are Inca roads—they simply could not be roads because of their size. I have photographs which show that these lines are about one sixth the width of a small teen-age girl standing with her feet together: I stress they are only about four to six inches in width—I will put a measure on one, take a photograph of it, and send it to you.

"To the person who knows the area, Von Daniken's pictures actually destroy all possibility of these being roads, but 'outsiders' would not know such things as these important points about the lines being extremely shallow and only a few inches wide.

"I have never seen a road that is not only four inches wide but also runs for about two miles and then just ends—a 'road' that has no beginning, no ending, and no place to go, like these endless lines. They merge into each other, run all around each other, and are continuous, like a figure 8.

"A number of the drawings on the ground are of plants known in the area, and that is illustrated by the figures showing llu llu. It is pronounced like 'yu yu,' and it is a kind of algae that grows in the ocean. The people eat it—we ourselves eat it in salads. It is depicted a number of times in these lines."

## Animistic Worship—Then and Now

"The fact that llu llu is drawn in these Nazca lines would indicate that it had a religious significance. To animists such as these people in Peru everything had religious significance. Everything around them is supposed to have a spiritual identity—if they get sick, they use certain herbs, administered by the witch doctor who uses his power to heal their sickness. People do not think of the chemical properties in the herbs as the means of healing their physical problems, but they believe that the spirit within the herbs will heal them.

"Even the earth itself is supposed to have divine attributes. One of our Christian women was pregnant, and she fell on the ground up in the mountains. She was a Quechua lady, and just before her baby was due to be born she developed a very bad boil in one of her breasts. She was some distance from her home at the time, being down in Nazca where we live. She was convinced that the only way she could be healed of that boil was to go back to the area where she had fallen, and to placate that piece of ground with a sacrifice. She believed that ground had some part of God in it, and so because she had disturbed it she must placate it if her boil was to be healed. She felt so badly about this that she actually made a pilgrimage back, to do just that.

"The Incas had a god Pachacamac whom they regarded as the god of the earth—the creator. These earlier people were also animists, and they believed there were evil spirits all around them. Even today when people in Peru are converted to Christianity we have to be careful to ensure that they move away from animistic practices, and begin to trust in the living God.

"I learned an interesting point about this from a witch doctor who was converted to Christianity. He had been a chief witch doctor in one of the towns on the Amazon, and his conversion gave a tremendous impetus to our work in that town. In my preaching I stressed to the people that it was quite all right for them to use herbs, barks of trees, and roots for medicinal purposes, but that they must recognize that those things should not be associated with the incantations of the witch doctors.

The point I stressed was that there was nothing wrong with using the plants because lots of them have real medicinal value, and people down there cannot always get laboratory help or drug store medicines. Often they are not available, and in any case they may not have the money to pay for such things. Thus I often told them that there was no reason why they should not use the actual herbs, and that they could avail themselves of the know-how of the witch doctor as to their proper use. My concern was that they should understand that there was no spiritual value in what the witch doctor was doing.

"After this chief witch doctor became a Christian, he told me that my approach was wrong: in using the herbs the people were not depending on the chemical properties of the herbs, or on the medicinal benefits within the herbs themselves, but on the spirit of that tree or herb from which the healing power came. They were actually depending on the spirit of that tree to heal them of their sickness.

"I had not understood that the people thought that way, and I did my utmost to clarify the situation from then on. The herbs had real value of course—as I often told the people, many of the medicines they bought from the drug stores came from those same herbs."

## That Trident on the Mountain

"Von Daniken also writes about other etchings in a mountainside not far from the Nazca lines. There is a sort of trident—having three separate lines, high up on the face of the cliff. Opinions vary about this. I have seen it, and my impression is that it depicts a cactus plant. The Incas drew pictures of plants they knew, and it looks like one of the many cactus plants growing wild down there. It looks like a single cactus, with the main stalk running up and the two branches stretching out on each side. It has no leaves, and this is typical of many of the cactuses down there.

"Not everyone would agree that it is a cactus plant: another view is that of Professor Garcia Montero, a Peruvian. He has studied these lines on the cliff, and he believes they are in the shape of a candelabra. He has written that the Bay of Pisco (really Paracas) was a known pirate haven, and he suggests that the pirates made this candlestick holder as a diversion. It is done in an entirely different manner from the Nazca lines.

"Professor Montero believes that this design high up on the cliffs shows a Catholic background. However, whether it is a candelabra or a cactus, it still would have religious significance. The candlestick is a church symbol, and a cactus would be linked with fertility rites and animism. As I say, I believe the sign depicts a cactus plant, and that it is associated with animistic worship or other forms of worship whose meaning is no longer understood.

"The fact of the actual construction of this 'sign' is not incredible. In *Crash Go the Chariots* you refer to other carvings high up the sides of mountains—such as those on the Behistun Rock, telling of the achievements of the ancient Persian king Darius the Great. Ancient rulers built all sorts of monuments, and probably this huge 'sign' in Peru had to do with the movements of heavenly bodies, so important in relation to planting and harvesting of crops. It is now common knowledge that many ancient people knew about equinoxes and solstices and other supposedly 'modern' concepts.

"Von Daniken suggested that this figure on the cliff was drawn for someone to see from the air, because it is so large. Perhaps he is close to the truth there, for these people worshipped heavenly bodies—the sun, the moon, and the stars. Possibly they were drawing it for their gods to see for some reason or another. As I have said, there was possibly some other religious significance whose meaning we no longer understand.

"Von Daniken believed it was significant that this rock carving pointed toward Nazca—Nazca has been an Indian center for many centuries. However, this 'sign' simply lies on the side of a hill, and I do not think there is any significance at all as to where it happens to point."

## The Nazca Lines, The Calendar, and Astronomy

"We mentioned that Maria Reiche has pointed out that the lines have astronomical significance—for instance, I have seen some that follow the pattern of the moon, and of particular stars.

"Sometimes in the afternoon as the sun goes down, its line can be traced right down one of the lines. I understand that every two months a different line follows the path of the sun as it moves to the south and then to the north, but I do not know the specific details. I personally have seen only two of these particular lines, but I understand there are six such lines associated with the sun's movements. This is a vast area of course.

"Not all scholars agree at this point. In his book *Beyond Stonehenge*, Gerald S. Hawkins gives the results of his use of a computer to attempt to position the lines with regard to stars and sun paths. He found that they do not significantly line up.

"We are not surprised that many of the lines do not line up with the movements of heavenly bodies, for—as we have seen—many of them depict animals, birds, constellations of the sky, and even local plants. However, it is also possible that some of the Nazca lines do depict a huge calendar of the skies.

"Alan and Sally Landsburg have a relevant comment about this:

> Furthermore, in 1941 Dr. Paul Kosok of Long Island University made a discovery about another line by playing a hunch. He thought the lines might have astronomical significance. So on June 22, the day of the winter solstice in the southern hemisphere, he stood in the desert and sighted along a line at sunset. The line pointed exactly to the sun as it touched the horizon. He was standing on a solstice line!
>
> Later he checked other lines and got readings understandable to an astronomer. They concerned paths of planets, the sun, the moon, and various stars. Working from the hypothesis that the chart had been laid out early in the sixth century, he found that a chart of the heavens as it then existed would have corresponded with many of the lines. He decided that the geometric figures in the desert might well be "the world's largest astronomy book." [2]

"Not only the Nazca lines, but also the fertility rites of the Incas, the planting of seeds, and the time of ploughing were all tied in with the calendar. Inca traditions certainly indicated that the heavenly bodies were very important in their daily lives.

"They even had a tradition about tying the sun down. This was at the time of the southern solstice.

When the sun reached its furthest southern point they performed this rite—the priests tied the sun so that it would not go any farther south. The sun was their god, and they did not want it to leave them. They would symbolically tie it down in their capital city, and they even had 'the hitching post of the sun' where they ceremonially tied it down on a certain day. Sure enough, the sun would then start moving north again—they knew the right day for this ceremony.

"To conclude: obviously these ancient people were capable of great achievements. However, what Von Daniken says about the Nazca lines cannot be taken seriously. This makes me doubt his other conclusions also. I agree with you that his chariots still crash."

## CHAPTER 8

# Epics of the Ancients

Erich Von Daniken has much to say about creation legends around the world—especially in his second book, *Gods from Outer Space*. He refers to legends from China, Easter Island, the ancient Indians, the Incas, the Mayas, the Polynesians, and others.[1] In this chapter we are especially interested in the ancient Sumerian legends, and he deals with some of them.

These people have been known by different names at different time periods—Akkadians, Sumerians, Babylonians, Chaldeans, and Mesopotamians. Mesopotamia means "between the rivers"—the rivers being the Euphrates and the Tigris. Today most of the area is in Iraq.

## History Repeating Itself

We shall consider some of the documents that are recorded on clay tablets from ancient Sumeria. As we put the translations alongside Von Daniken's comments, it almost seems as though history is repeating itself from 100 years ago. At that time also the genuineness of the Genesis records as original documents was challenged.

The story is quite dramatic. In 1872 George Smith of the British Museum had published a translation of fragments of the Babylonian Flood story, and it had caught the imagination of the public. An English newspaper eventually arranged for him to go out to Nineveh to find the missing parts of the story. This was an incredible assignment, with an extremely small chance of success, but the amazing fact is that George Smith found what he was looking for—Assyrian copies of Babylonian records relating to Creation and the Flood.

Then in 1876 Smith published his *Chaldean Account of Genesis,* and scholars claimed that they now had a record of creation pre-dating the one in the Bible, and that the Bible story was based on the Babylonian record. Later investigations revealed that in the seventh century B.C. the famous Assyrian king Ashurbanipal had sent scribes all over the ancient world collecting documents, especially from foundations of buildings and ancient libraries. Many were recovered from the temples of his southern neighbors, the Babylonians. Ashurbanipal amassed over 20,000 clay tablets, and among them were the Assyrian translations of the Babylonian creation and flood stories.

These tablets from Ashurbanipal's palace dated to about 650 B.C., and earlier copies have since been found, but they are essentially the same. One series recounts a legend that goes back to the beginning of Creation, and the other tells the story of the Flood. There were many other records, but Western scholars have found these two especially important. The Creation record is known as *Enuma Elish,* which literally means "when above"—these being the first two words of this epic poem about Creation. The best-known Flood story is part of the Epic of Gilgamesh.[2]

## The Battle of the Gods

The *Enuma Elish* has about a thousand lines, and is on seven clay tablets. The narrative states that in the beginning there existed only the god Apsu, who was supposed to be the male personification of the freshwater ocean, and the goddess Tiamut, a female personification of the saltwater ocean. They created many other gods, but these displeased Apsu and he decided to kill them all off. One god, Ea, became aware of the plan, so he got in first and killed Apsu. Then Ea himself begat another god, Marduk, who was the patron god of Babylon. Now it was Tiamut's turn, and she determined to avenge the death of her husband. She created other monster gods, and put one of these newly created gods called Kingu at their head.

Eventually fighting broke out among the gods when the goddess Tiamut and her group of rebel deities prepared for total war against the prevailing gods. At first Tiamut was successful against the gods Ea and Enu, but then the powerful young god Marduk was proclaimed king of the gods. Soon he had defeated Tiamut and cut her in two, then forced the rebel gods into servitude. Consequently Marduk was confirmed as king in the assembly of the gods—"the king of the gods of heaven and earth, the king of all the gods."

In describing Marduk's successful battle against Tiamut, the grotesque language used points to the inhuman practices ascribed to Babylonian gods. Having shot the arrow which pierced Tiamut's mouth, her stomach, and her intestines, Marduk rested for a while, and then he conceived the idea of creating a new heaven. He examined her body, then "slit her in two like a fish in the drying yard." One half of her body he used to make the sky, and from this he traced out the paths of the gods of the heavens, then determined the seasons of the year. The sun and the moon had special positions of control over the day and the night, respectively. These ancient people attached great importance to the heavenly bodies and their relationships to times and seasons.

## The Euphrates and the Tigris Flow Through Tiamut's Eyes

The story goes on to show how Marduk reshaped the earth out of the lower half of Tiamut's body, after the Euphrates and Tigris Rivers had been made to flow through her eyes. Then followed an assembly of the rebel gods who did obeisance and fully recognized Marduk as their king.

This is all very different from the record in the early chapters of Genesis. There we do not read of gods fighting, or of immoral activity, or of primitive super-stitious nonsense whereby two rivers flow through the eyes of a goddess. The Bible account is dignified and noble, and can be believed as a record of divine activity provided we accept the concept of the one true God Who is all-powerful, able to create from nothing.

The Bible concept of God's purpose in the creation of man is also very different. In the Babylonian account man is to be merely a slave, brought into being by Marduk at the plea of the defeated rebel gods, so that those gods themselves need not be subjected to servile labor—man would be a puppet, a lowly, primitive creature.[3] The Bible presents a much nobler concept, and speaks of man made in the image of God, able to live in fellowship with God.

The Babylonian story tells how the gods persuaded Marduk against his plans of making man for such an entirely lowly purpose, which was really a form of punishment. They suggested instead that the god Kingu, who incited Tiamut to revolt, should be punished. Thus Kingu was bound and the crime was blamed on him, and the punishment included his cutting his own throat. Marduk then created man from Kingu's blood instead of from nothing as originally planned. Thus the evil Kingu, the chief of the rebels against divine authority, bore the full punishment of the revolt. It followed that man, as the offspring of Kingu—made from his blood—could only be evil, and must be subject to every whim of the gods.

## Gods, Not Men, Created

In the Babylonian story the gods, not men, are

created. Instead of God making man in His own image, man makes corrupt gods after his own image.

The penalties against the rebel gods were ultimately revoked, and the rebels were given the task of rebuilding Babylon. Soon they sought permission to make great changes in the original plans, so that Babylon would not only be Marduk's home, but would also be a great religious sanctuary for gods and men alike. Permission was given, and the great temple of Marduk was built at Babylon.

This highlights another difference between the *Enuma Elish* and the Bible account—this Assyrian copy of the Babylonian epic was clearly political in purpose, showing why Babylon should be accepted as the leading city because it was the home of the great god Marduk. When a later Assyrian account was subsequently recovered it was found that the name of the Assyrian god Ashur had been substituted for Marduk: the political purpose was to demonstrate the supremacy of the Assyrian city of Ashur, which was named after that god.

When Marduk was confirmed by the full assembly of gods as king forever, the other gods yielded him homage. They swore their loyalty in blood drained from their own throats, yielding him eternal power to rule over them as king. They recognized that "his command shall be pre-eminent above and below." In the Bible, God is eternal, whereas the Babylonian Marduk had to be brought into existence by an act of creation, then later he was made eternal.

Another recently translated Babylonian record of creation is the Epic of Atrahasis. Until 1965 only about one fifth of this was known, but now about four fifths have been restored. It dates to about 1630 B.C., and fragmentary copies of it were found in the Assyrian libraries of Nineveh, dating about 1,000 years later. Other fragments have been found at Babylon, at

Nippur, and at the ancient Hittite capital of Bogazköy —this last copy dates to about 1000 B.C.

An interesting point of comparison with the biblical record is that this is the only known Babylonian epic in which a continuous narrative is given covering the first era of human existence—until now, scholars have usually looked on the Creation and Flood stories as separate records.

## Man Created to Save the Gods from Working

In similar vein to the *Enuma Elish,* one of the main ideals underlying the Atrahasis Epic is to show why man was created by the gods—it was so that they themselves need not work on the earth to produce their own food. Some scholars have suggested that this same thought is carried over into the biblical account where man is put into a garden which he is to tend, but there is an essential difference. According to the biblical account, man is not created to feed the gods, but he is put into a garden where he will know the dignity of work.

Another similarity between the *Enuma Elish* and the Atrahasis Epic is in the making of man. In both epics a god is slaughtered, and his blood was one of the elements from which man was formed. The Epic of Atrahasis is supposed to have similarities to the Genesis record, as to the use of clay and man being made in the image of a god, but the most that could be said is that both Babylonian epics are gross distortions of the original. As we study these other records and compare them with the Bible record, it becomes clear that the only version that could be accepted as the original is in the early chapters of Genesis.

## Man's Noise Interrupts the Sleep of a God

The Epic of Atrahasis also tells of men multiplying on the earth, and the great god Enlil was annoyed because of the noise they made—it was so great that he was losing his sleep. A series of visitations against mankind followed, with Enlil seeking to destroy man while the God Enki who had created him sought to protect him.

Man's noise continued to annoy Enlil, and a flood was sent on the earth. The god Enki was able to intervene for his special devotee Atrahasis—the Babylonian Noah—and he was saved from destruction.

When the Flood ended, Atrahasis, like Utnapishtim in the Epic of Gilgamesh, offered sacrifices to the gods. They were hungry because men had not fed them during the time of the flood.

After the Flood, the gods resolved to control the number of mankind, and this dimly reminds us of the statement in Genesis that man's days would be limited from the time of the Flood onward. Other points of similarity include the ark being used to save representative man, the sending out of birds, the ark being grounded on a mountain, and a man sacrificing after he had come out of the ark.

## The Embellishment of Legends

As one compares this epic and other legends with the Genesis records, the superiority of the Bible record soon becomes apparent. However, to some people the question then arises: "Are the Genesis records the result of intensive revision and adjustment so that more enlightened people can accept them as God-given?" An excellent answer is given by A. R. Millard. He surveyed this new Babylonian story and concluded:

> All who suspect or suggest borrowing by the Hebrews are compelled to admit large-scale revision, alteration, and reinterpretation in a fashion which cannot be substantiated for any other composition from the ancient Near East or in any other Hebrew writing. . . . Careful comparison

of ancient texts and literary methods is the only
way to the understanding of the early chapters of
Genesis. Discovery of new material requires re-
assessment of former conclusions; so the Epic of
Atrahasis adds to knowledge of parallel Babylonian traditions, and of their literary form. All
speculation apart, it underlines the uniqueness of
the Hebrew primaeval history in the form in which
it now exists.[4]

There are both similarities and differences between
Babylonian accounts of Creation and that found in the
Bible. The similarities suggest a common source—clay
is associated with the creation of man, and possibly
the fact of seven tablets has some relationship to the
seven days of Creation in the Bible, especially as the
creation of man appears on the sixth of the Babylonian
tablets and man is created on the sixth day in the Bible
story. However, on purely academic grounds, if we are
to choose an original from these two old documents
the Bible record must be selected. It does not allow for
polytheism or crude mythology, or for grotesque
amoral activity, as in the Babylonian epics.

The comment of Kenneth Kitchen of the University
of Liverpool is relevant as a conclusion at this point:

The common assumption that the Hebrew account is simply a purged and simplified version of
the Babylonian legend (applied also to the Flood
stories) is fallacious on methodological grounds.
In the Ancient Near East, the rule is that simple
accounts or traditions may give rise (by accretion
and embellishment) to elaborate legends, but not
vice versa. In the Ancient Orient, legends were
not simplified or turned into pseudo-history (his-
toricized) as has been assumed for early Genesis.[5]

We started this chapter with a reference to George
Smith's *Chaldean Account of Genesis*. It did not finally
destroy the Bible after all, for continuing study has

shown that the Chaldean records are grotesque distortions, clearly inferior to the records of Genesis.

## A Poem about the Garden of Eden?

Another ancient Sumerian tablet has interesting similarities to the biblical account of the Garden of Eden, in a poem known as the Epic of Emmerkar.[6] This epic talked about the land Dilmun—it was a clean and pure place, where the lion did not kill and the lamb and the wolf were peacefully associated. Sickness was unknown, and in these and other ways this land had interesting similarities to the biblical Garden of Eden.

The land of Dilmun was traditionally close to the general area of the Persian Gulf, and it was said to be irrigated by fresh water. This is somewhat like the words of Genesis 2:6 which speaks of a water source independent of rain. The epic says that even birth was originally without distress, until Enki ate eight plants which involved a deadly curse. This is clearly similar to Adam and Eve partaking of the forbidden fruit, with a curse resulting.

Yet another tablet describes the special act whereby woman was created. She is called "Nin.ti," a Sumerian expression which can be equally translated "The lady of the rib" and "The lady who makes live." According to Professor D. J. Wiseman's translation, this recalls Eve, the mother of all living, fashioned from Adam.[7]

## Early Civilizations and the Bible

Another interesting point is that the Bible touches briefly on civilizations that were thriving before the Flood.

In Genesis, chapter 4, we read about the man Cain who went and lived in the Land of Nod, and we are told that he built a town (Genesis 4:17). In that same chapter we read of people who played on harps and flutes, and of another man named Tubal-Cain who was a smith, able to make all sorts of sharp tools of bronze and iron. The next chapter speaks of shepherds, cattlemen, nomads, and farmers. This indicates that both settled and more nomadic types of life were contemporary long before the biblical flood.

We cannot say because of these somewhat isolated clues that the Bible offers conclusive evidence of extensive earlier civilizations. What we can say is that the Bible does not exclude such possibilities. The Bible references indicate there were workers in iron long before the so-called iron age of archaeology; just as clearly there were established civilizations before the biblical Flood. It is by no means impossible that some of those men of renown who are listed in Genesis could have established great cities, and invented highly advanced technological methods and equipment, and migrated to areas which were a considerable distance from the land between the two rivers.

From time to time there are interesting discoveries made by archaeologists which throw light on some of these isolated comments—thus we know that copper was fairly common about 4000 B.C., for it was found to have been used at Halaf and Chagar Bazar in northwest Mesopotamia. Similarly, iron was used at the ancient site of Eshnunna, just outside Baghdad, about 2500 B.C.—a bronze knife was found with the blade missing, but with some corroded metal still in the handle. When this was analyzed, it was found to be iron.

## Men Who Lived for Hundreds of Years

Another point about these early civilizations before the Flood is that the Bible gives a list of men who lived for very long periods—hundreds of years.

We learn from archaeology that there are traditions about men living for great lengths of time, and there is evidence of a historical basis for those traditions. The so-called Sumerian King List tells of long-living kings who lived "before the Flood." According to the ancient historian Berossus, those kings reigned for periods ranging from 10,800 years to 64,800 years each, and the grand total is 432,000. By comparison with these great periods of time, the Bible figures are not so strange after all. Obviously we do not accept those Babylonian figures, but when we put them alongside the Bible statements we are impressed with the conservative nature of the Bible record.

This tradition that men lived for long periods of time is known to many peoples. The Egyptians and the Chinese speak of kings who lived for thousands of years. The later Greeks and Romans were more conservative than the Babylonians in their figures, for they suggested ages from 800 to 1,000 years, reminding us of the Bible figures. The Jewish historian Josephus, who lived at the time of Christ, apparently had no doubts about the authenticity of these long-living early men, and he wrote accepting the traditions of various peoples who united their testimony to this as fact.

The fact that we today do not live for 800 or 900 years does not mean that such longevity was never possible. We do not know what tremendous climatic or other changes occurred when the biblical Flood took place. We do not know what cataclysmic effects it would have had on past civilizations and cultures—perhaps virtually wiping out all traces of such culture. It could possibly have caused the great climatic changes of which we have clues when we find there was tropical growth at the South Pole, and that the Siberian wastelands of today once were able to provide food for huge mammals.

Some of these have been found in recent times with great quantities of grass and vegetation still undigested. There are reputable scholars who seriously suggest that they were suddenly overtaken, possibly by the Flood described in detail in the Bible, at Genesis chapters 7 through 9.

It is interesting to notice that the long ages of the Sumerian King List are suddenly reduced after the Flood to about 100 years—and we find a somewhat similar decrease in longevity in the Bible records relating to pre- and post-Flood conditions.

The record in the Bible of the Flood also has some interesting possibilities—we learn that God is about to destroy not only mankind, but the earth itself, and in Genesis 7:11 we read that all the fountains of the great deep broke through and all the sluices of heaven were opened up. This was not only a great deluge, but also something affecting the very fountains of the great deep, whatever that might mean. Volumes have been written to suggest that this could involve releasing of water from the poles, great earthquake activity, and other changes involving even the tilt of the axis of the earth so that great climatic changes should possibly be traced to this time of the biblical Flood.

## The Babylonian Epic of Gilgamesh

The best known of the Babylonian records of the Flood is in the Epic of Gilgamesh. Gilgamesh himself was the legendary ruler of the ancient city-state of Uruk, and he was supposed to be two-thirds god and one-third man.

The story of the Flood is told on the eleventh of the twelve tablets making up the epic. Utnapishtim was the Babylonian Noah, and with his boatman Puzur-Amurri he went through seven days of terrible flood. Enkidu, the very good friend of Gilgamesh, had died at the decree of the gods, and Gilgamesh realized that he too must eventually die. He hears of one who has escaped death and sets off to find him, so that he can learn the secret of immortality. Alongside a great sea he meets Siduri the Ale-wife: it is she who provides the beer needed for travelers on the sea. After crossing this sea, known as the "waters of death," he at last finds Utnapishtim, the only man who had ever found everlasting life.

Utnapishtim speaks to Gilgamesh, and learns of his sadness at the death of his friend Enkidu, and of his sorrow as he wandered up and down pondering the great mystery of life and death. Gilgamesh asks Utnapishtim how he had come to stand in the assembly of the gods and find everlasting life. Utnapishtim then tells the story of how one of the gods urged him to destroy his house, and to build a vessel into which he was to bring representative living creatures.

The epic tells in detail how Utnapishtim built a great boat which needed 30,000 baskets of pitch, and the great flood came after he and his family were safely aboard.

So terrible was the storm that "even the gods were afeared at the deluge, took to flight and went up to the heaven of Anu, cowered they like dogs and crouched down at the outer defenses." The goddess Ashtar wept at the calamity—"cried like a woman in travail, wailed the queen of the gods with her beautiful voice."

Utnapishtim rode out the storm, then waited several days for the waters to abate. On the seventh day he freed a dove which flew around for a while, then came back. Next he sent forth a swallow which also came back. Then a raven was released, but the raven "saw again the natural flowing of the waters, and he ate and he flew about and he croaked, and came not returning."

### "The Gods Gathered like Flies"

The waters were now swiftly abating, and eventually Utnapishtim came out from his great vessel. He poured out a libation to the gods, then made an offering for them—

And the gods smelled the savour, the gods smelled the sweet savour, the gods gathered like flies about the priest of the offering.[8]

These poor gods had not been fed, because mankind had been destroyed. So they gathered like flies as soon as Utnapishtim remembered their need and did something about it.

Then we read of gods angry with each other. The god Enlil is furious against the other gods and demands, "Has ought of living-kind escaped? Not a man should have survived the destruction!" The gods were not one in their purpose, and that was shown by Utnapishtim surviving the judgment. He escaped it because one of those very gods had given him warning.

Then, according to Utnapishtim, the god Ea suggested that Enlil had indiscriminately brought about the deluge. He argued that only those who had sinned should have been judged, and that, instead of a flood, animals such as lions and wolves should have been used; or a famine would have been sufficient punishment, for this would have impoverished but not destroyed mankind.

Enlil listened to Ea's reasoning, and then he came to Utnapishtim and his wife and decreed that they would henceforth be as one of the gods, dwelling in the "Far Distance, at the Mouth of the Rivers."

Obviously much of this is very different from the God of the Bible—He would not "cower like a dog," or be "afeared at the deluge"; He does not need the offerings of a man to sate His hunger, nor could we imagine the God of Heaven coming "like flies to an offering." Nor was there disharmony as to the divine judgment. When mercy was rejected, God's judgment fell—a consistent Bible picture.

## Von Daniken's Strange Theories

Erich Von Daniken discusses this famous Epic of

Gilgamesh at considerable length. As with so many of his statements, he is confused, this time as to the origin of the epic. At one point he tells us: "It is an established fact that the original version of the Epic of Gilgamesh stems from the Sumerians." [9] However, only four pages later in this book he asks us, "Is it possible that the Epic of Gilgamesh did not originate in the ancient East at all but in the Tiahuanaco region? Is it conceivable that the descendants of Gilgamesh came from South America and brought the epic with them?" [10]

He is also confused as to where the boat landed, apparently not realizing that the biblical and Babylonian accounts differ at this point. He tells us that "ancient Babylonian cuneiform texts indicate very precisely where the remains of the boat ought to be" and he goes on to talk about Mount Ararat.[11] Actually the Epic of Gilgamesh does not say that the ark landed on Mount Ararat, but on Mount Nisir.[12] Von Daniken has confused the biblical Mount Ararat with Mount Nisir of the Babylonian epic.

Some of Von Daniken's other statements about this epic are amazingly divorced from facts: he tells us that "it is also clear that the main thread of the Epic of Gilgamesh runs parallel to the biblical Book of Genesis." The Epic of Gilgamesh has some similarities to (and also great dissimilarities from) the biblical story of the Flood. However, from chapter 12 onward, the Book of Genesis is dealing with Abraham and the other patriarchs of Israel—it certainly is not a parallel to the Epic of Gilgamesh.

When we read on and find that Von Daniken suggests that the record of Exodus also possibly had its origins in the Epic of Gilgamesh, we hardly know what to say. Von Daniken's hypothesis is nonsensical: the Book of Exodus is dealing with the nation of Israel coming out from Egypt, and it tells of their journey toward Canaan, the promised land that was eventually to be known as Israel. The Book of Exodus clearly did not originate from the Babylonian Epic of Gilgamesh.

At a more sensible level, Von Daniken tells us, "The parallel between the stories of the Flood in the Epic of Gilgamesh and the Bible is beyond doubt, and there is not a single scholar who contests it." [13] He suggests the possibility that the account of the Flood in the Bible is a secondhand one, the Babylonian epic being the "firsthand report." [14]

Again he becomes confusing, for if the Epic of Gilgamesh is the firsthand account, the original, we cannot understand how he is giving us the facts when he states concerning a more recently found flood account, "So we now possess an even older description of the Flood than the one in the Epic of Gilgamesh. No one knows whether new finds will not produce still earlier accounts." [15]

How can the Epic of Gilgamesh be the "firsthand report" when there is now "an even older description"? We shall see that the evidence suggests that the oldest account of the Flood is in the Bible.

## Similarities to, and Differences from the Bible

As with the Epic of Atrahasis, scholars have pointed to some similarities in the Epic of Gilgamesh to the Bible story: thus in each record there is supposedly a final revelation to the hero of the Flood, warning him that a deluge is coming which is unknown to everyone else. However, in the Bible story, Noah is told to warn others so that they, too, can accept the way of escape if they so desire. It is not so in the Babylonian epic.

In each case the hero builds a vessel which is sealed inside and outside with pitch; it describes the flood in which all other people are destroyed; it tells of the great ship resting on a mountain, and of certain birds being sent out. Each record tells how the hero disembarks and offers a sacrifice, and then it affirms that such a deluge shall not be visited on man again.

There are other Babylonian flood records, such as that written on a tablet at Nippur and dating before 2000 B.C., but, as with the Epic of Gilgamesh, the Bible record is invariably superior. It does not bear the marks of the grotesque, or the superstitious, or the magical.

A copy of part of the Epic of Gilgamesh was found in the excavations at Megiddo in ancient Palestine (now Israel). It was nearly a thousand years earlier than the copy found in the palace of the Assyrian king Ashurbanipal, and it showed that the story was widely known throughout the entire East.

Someone who traveled the long route from Babylon to Palestine must have taken that clay tablet with him. If that could be done with other ancient stories known in Babylonia, it could be true of Bible stories also. Abraham migrated across that same "Fertile Crescent" from Ur to Canaan, not so very long before the date of this particular copy of the Babylonian flood story, and he could well have carried the original tablets which Moses eventually used to give us the early stories in Genesis.

Such a possibility has been developed by P. J. Wiseman in his fascinating book, *New Discoveries in Babylonia about Genesis.* He put forward the argument that the literary aids demonstrated in Genesis indicate "that the book was compiled at an early date, certainly not later than the age of Moses." He suggested that the repetition of words and phrases pointed to different clay tablets, the first words of the new tablet being a repetition of the last words of the previous record—what is sometimes called a "colophon." [16] He adds convincing evidence to show similar practices from the written records of the ancient East—he demonstrates that the early Bible records in Genesis follow the recognized pattern.

Obviously the Bible records did not come from South America! Nor were they copied from the clay tablets recovered in the palace of Ashurbanipal. As Professor W. F. Albright points out, "The Bible record contains archaic features dating it to before any Mesopotamian version that is 'preserved in cuneiform sources.'" [17]

## The Confusion of Tongues

One other Sumerian epic poem should be mentioned. The March, 1968, *Journal of the American Oriental Society* consists of a series of essays in memory of the famous archaeologist E. A. Speiser. One essay is by Professor S. N. Kramer, of the University of Pennsylvania, and it is entitled, "The 'Babel of Tongues'—A Sumerian Version." Dr. Kramer reminds us that E. A. Speiser analyzed with characteristic acumen, learning, and skill, the Mesopotamian background of the "Tower of Babel" narrative, and came to the conclusion that it "had a demonstrable source in cuneiform literature." [18]

Professor Speiser was by no means alone in this view: Professor Robert Braidwood was another who referred to the widespread recognition of the factual basis of some early civilizations that had previously been regarded as purely mythical.

Dr. Kramer says of his own article: "This paper will help to corroborate and confirm Speiser's conclusion by bringing to light a new parallel to one of the essential motifs in the 'Tower of Babel' theme—the confusion of tongues."

## A Golden Age—One Language

Another essay in this same series tells of a fragmentary tablet of twenty-seven lines that has recently been copied by the Oxford cuneiformist Oliver Gurney. This helps to restore the idea of a "Golden Age," an idea known in literature for about twenty-five years.

This Golden Age was supposed to have been part of the earlier Sumerian period. The new fragmentary tablet includes a Sumerian version of the story of the confusion of tongues.

Here is part of the translation as it relates to this Sumerian version of the time when there was only one language, in a land without sadness or fear:

Once upon a time there was no snake, there was
  no scorpion,
There was no hyena, there was no lion,
There was no wild dog, no wolf. There was no fear,
  no terror.

Man had no rival.
In those days, the lands Subur and Hamazi,
Harmony-tongued Sumer, the great land of the de-
  crees of princeship,
Uri, the land having all that is appropriate.
The land Martu, resting in security,
The whole universe, the people in unison
To Enlil in one tongue . . .[19]

Clearly men believed in a Golden Age when they were free from fear and want, living in a world that knew nothing but prosperity—a veritable Garden of Eden. All the people of the world worshipped one god, it being claimed in this story that he was the Sumerian god Enlil. They were able to speak to their god in one tongue, as we are told in the last line above.

This was not the first tablet recovered with a reference to speaking in one tongue: in fact, this new tablet is actually a better preserved copy of the previously known epic tale "Enmerkar and the Lord of Aratta," published by Dr. Kramer in 1952 as a monograph of the University of Pennsylvania Museum. However, until this new tablet was translated, the meaning of parts of that epic was ambiguous—it could have been taken literally to suggest that all the peoples of the world did use the same language, or it could have been looked at as a figurative expression declaring the unanimity of of all people as they acknowledged the supremacy of Enlil. This new text makes it clear that people were indeed supposed to speak but one language.

As Dr. Kramer says:

> Our new piece, therefore, puts it beyond all doubt that the Sumerians believed that there was a time when all mankind spoke one and the same language, and that it was Enki, the Sumerian god of wisdom, who confounded their speech. The reason for this fateful deed is not stated in the text; it may well have been inspired by Enki's jealousy of Enlil and the universal sway over mankind that he enjoyed.[20]

## The Tower of Babel and Languages

Professor W. F. Albright suggested that the story of the Tower of Babel itself should be dated to the twenty-second century B.C., and in a discussion of some of the terminology in the Bible record he concluded, "It was, therefore, as a tremendous monument to its builders that the Tower of Babel was intended." [21] He took the record seriously.

There are a number of traditions around the world as to the building of the Tower of Babel being linked with the confusion of man's language. Robert T. Boyd has an especially interesting comment on this:

> Not only has the discovery of many "ziggurats" helped to confirm the biblical record of a tower at Babel, but further evidence relates a story of king Ur-Nammu of the Third Dynasty of Ur (2044 to 2007 B.C.). He received orders from his god and goddess to build the ziggurat. The stele is nearly five feet across and ten feet high. At the top, the king stands in an attitude of prayer. Above his

head is the symbol of the moon god Nannar and to the right are figures of angels, with vases from which flow the streams of life (the earliest known artistic figures of angels). The panels show the king setting out with compass, pick, and trowel, and mortar baskets to begin construction. One panel preserves only a ladder used as the structure was rising. The reverse side records a commemorative feast.[22]

The date given is interesting—in the twenty-first century B.C. As seen above, Albright had suggested the twenty-second century. Dating that extends back into the third millennia B.C. is not yet exact, and this is an interesting approximation. Traditions such as this have bases in fact, and a surprising number of "new" civilizations that suddenly appear are dated to approximately 2000 B.C. It may be more than coincidence.

## *"Their Speech Was Strange"*

In the same context, Robert Boyd goes on:

A clay tablet was unearthed which gave the following account of a ziggurat: "The erection (building) of this tower (temple) highly offended all the gods. In a night they (threw down) what man had built, and impeded their progress. They were scattered abroad, and their speech was strange." Once again the archaeologist has given to us evidence that the Bible records and accounts of other peoples of other nations are closely related, and that the Bible is not just a "one-sided" account of events and happenings.

Not all will accept the spiritual overtones of this interpretation, nor agree with an extremely literal interpretation of the Bible record at this point. However, the fact is that there has been a great change of scholarly

## A Consistent Pattern in Ancient Tablets

thinking about some sudden happening, and a consequent dispersion of culture and of language.

Summarizing these points, an interesting pattern emerges from the study of recovered Sumerian tablets. Those stories that are preserved tell of gods creating heaven and earth, of man coming directly from the gods, of man being immediately intelligent and civilized, of disease not being present, of plentiful food in a garden, and animals at peace in that garden. Man offends the gods and is expelled from the garden, with misery and sorrow following.

Men live for very long periods, but eventually a great flood destroys almost all of mankind. One survivor pleases the Divine powers, and his offering is accepted. As time passes, men build cities and use bronze and iron implements.

As their prowess increases, so does their pride. They set out to build a huge tower that will reach into the heavens, and this displeases the gods. Men are scattered across the face of the earth, and their language is confounded. . . . So the Sumerian tablets tell us, and a number of those traditions are known also in other parts of the earth.

Despite the polytheism in some of the Sumerian tablets, they have so much similarity to the record in Genesis that it is reasonable to assume that the Bible stories are far more factual than many scholars of a previous generation would have acknowledged.

It is usually conceded that when different races have a common idea that is strongly developed, there is a basis of truth, or an historical incident, at the source of that belief. Thus there is increasing recognition that the Genesis records are set in a historical framework.

A relevant comment comes from Professor G. Ernest Wright of Harvard:

Consequently, an increasing number of scholars have been coming to the conclusion that many of these ancient traditions regarding origins must go back to an earlier period. In fact, it seems most probable that some of the traditions about the Creation, the Garden of Eden, the Flood, the stories of Nimrod (Genesis 10:8 ff.) and of the Tower of Babel (Genesis 11) were brought from Mesopotamia by the Patriarchs themselves. How else explain why Israel had them but Canaan did not? [23]

It is also thought-provoking to realize that no historical records have been found of people who claimed that their beginnings were by descent or ascent from lower forms of life. In these ancient epics the gods might be created in the forms of men, but men are never created in forms such as the serpent god, the monkey god, or the cow god.

## CHAPTER 9

# The Gospel Not
# According to Von Daniken

It would not be desirable to reproduce in this second book everything that has already been published in *Crash Go the Chariots*. On the other hand, I am constantly asked many questions that are touched on in that book. As we said in the introduction, it is no longer readily available.

When Jack Powell, managing director of K-JAY radio in Sacramento, California, asked me a series of quick-fire questions on his "V.I.P." program, an idea was born. It was one of the smoothest radio interviews I have ever been involved in—Jack asked the questions, allowed me to present only the main points in answering, then moved into his next question. A lot of ground was covered in a short time. I asked him if I could use the tape, and he willingly gave permission for me to do as I liked with it.

I have taken some of that material and added a number of other questions that have been asked on talk shows and at public meetings. I have now edited the material and adapted it for inclusion as a chapter summarizing a number of questions still being asked. The continuing interest is very real.

## From Faith to Phantasy

QUESTION: Is Von Daniken in touch with powers beyond this planet Earth?

ANSWER: *Encounter* magazine for August, 1973, analyzes Von Daniken's success. Under the heading, "From Jesus to the Astronauts," it states that Von Daniken's conversion from the faith of Jesus to that of the astronauts "began with a vision—or a process

146

of extrasensory perception—which he subsequently christened *Espern,* a German verbalization of the initials ESP. Daniken now submits that it was his first ESP experience in spring 1954 which convinced him of a prehistoric earth-landing by astronauts from outer space. From then on, he was enabled, in fact impelled, to go in search of the traces left by his gods.[1]

QUESTION: Does he give examples of this supposed knowledge?

ANSWER: In one of the *Encounter* interviews he stated that he knew his book would be a huge success long before its publication. He was asked if extrasensory perception was a major source of his knowledge and in his answer he referred to "a source which led me to the firm belief that the earth had been visited by extraterrestrial astronauts. I know this. I also know that an event will take place in the near future which will prove I'm right." [2] Von Daniken describes his "ESP" as a sort of journey through time. He "steps out of time" and sees "everything simultaneously— past, present, and future." He converses with "people from the past" who possess the "same faculty" as he does; he knows the date of his next book and the manner of his own death.[3]

## An Absorbing Interest in Life's Origins

QUESTION: At page 58 of *The Gold of the Gods* Von Daniken asks, "Can't we bury the old Adam as 'Lord of Creation' once and for all?" What do you think?

ANSWER: In his books Von Daniken shows an absorbing interest in the origin of life—in fact, one of the main objectives of *The Gold of the Gods* was to reveal that the purpose of creation was written on metal plates supposedly found in Ecuador. The plates have never been photographed, and no normally acceptable evidence has been presented to demonstrate their existence. It was "gold of the gods" —a "golden" opportunity to "bury the old Adam as 'Lord of Creation' once and for all." Like so many similar efforts through the centuries, it has failed.

QUESTION: Do space writers seriously believe in life on earth resulting from a visit of beings from another planet?

ANSWER: I discuss this in my book *UFOs and Their Mission Impossible*. There I state that many ufologists (students of UFO activities) believe this theory, for they reject the biblical concept of special creation. It then follows that because Darwinian and succeeding theories of evolution have become increasingly untenable, an alternative should be advanced. Thus they put forward supposed evidence that Homo sapiens is descended from spacemen who visited the earth in ancient times. They point out that it is impossible to interbreed a man and an ape, and discuss the fact that man alone has a sense of destiny and a religious capacity. Typical writers along this line are Otto Binder and Max H. Flindt. They are not setting out to prove a biblical viewpoint as to man's creation, but are simply arguing that the riddle of man is resolved by seeing man's ancestors as coming from the stars.

Many ufologists believe that original man was created by a union of these beings from other planets with lower creatures on earth, and one argument commonly put forward by ufologists is that modern man could not have evolved on the earth without some outside assistance. Otto Binder submits a number of points to show that man could not merely be a product of evolution on the earth. He quotes liberally from Max H. Flindt, *On Tip-Toe Beyond Darwin,* and elaborates the hypothesis that possibly one or more of our ancestors came from outer space.

QUESTION: Do they really believe this story?

ANSWER: Binder submits that Flindt's argument is an answer to problems of evolution, claiming that the Darwinian-based hypothesis is unable to give satisfactory answers. We quote Binder as typical of the theories of a number of space writers at this point: [4]

As stated before, Darwin himself admitted at times that mankind in small ways fitted his evolution theory the least of all creatures. Alfred Wallace, his contemporary formulator of the theory of evolution, was even more emphatic, and forthrightly said that man was an exception to the orderly operation of biological laws, and that natural selection could not have operated in his case. What the true answer was he hazarded no guess.

Binder then quotes Flindt's theory as to man coming from a union between beings from the stars and earth creatures: [5]

And Flindt does give the answer that Wallace was unable to find, as a succinct question—"Is it because man's brain is an import?"

Namely, that man appeared so suddenly on the scene because he was a planned hybrid, a cross between super-intelligent star men and subintelligent two-legged creatures on earth.

## Man's Uniqueness

QUESTION: Do these writers elaborate the ways in which man is unique?

ANSWER: Later in his comments on this topic, Binder gives a list of the ways in which he claims man is unique and different from other creatures. He states that only man cries; that among the primates only man has bushy hair on top of his skull; that man has almost no body hair, whereas other creatures are hairy; that man alone possesses a supersensitive skin with a fine sense of touch which is denied to animals; that this last means that so much more information can be sent to a human brain because of stimuli to skin; that man swallows slowly, whereas with animals such as dogs food is virtually shot from the esophagus into the stomach; that man lacks tooth gaps; he does not have the penis bone that is associated with mammals and animals—a bone that rises within the penis before and during the sex act, whereas with human males emotion and blood supply are involved rather than a special bone. He refers also to the fact that the fertilized ovum of the human female is quite different from that of any other being, in that it buries itself in the woman's uterus wall.

He goes on to discuss the very great differences relating to the brain and "imported mentality." He also discusses the impossibility of interbreeding man with apes or other animals.

QUESTION: What does he say about the human brain?

ANSWER: He refers to ancient men, many thousands of years before modern men, having a bigger brain capacity than modern man. This early "large brained sub-man" was one of our immediate ancestors, with a brain capacity three times that of a gorilla. His brain capacity is also three times that of other animals in proportion to their body weight, with a very much greater thinking capacity. He suggests that possibly this is the result of an interbreeding program with spacemen.

Until writings such as these began to be prominent in recent times, most of the forthright opposition to the Darwin-based theory of evolution came from Christians who saw it as opposing the Bible. Now many ufologists reject Darwin and the later developments of that theory on biological and other grounds.

QUESTION: Is it not a chemical problem also?

ANSWER: Yes, it certainly should be recognized as a chemical problem. It is not simply a matter of deciding what processes should be selected, for there are basic restrictions on chemical molecules, as to the forms into which they can develop physically and biologically. The arrangement of chemical molecules is fantastically complex, and to suggest that they have been arranged into entirely new formations without any supervision or proper control, with no "intelligence" behind their organization, is virtually incredible. Such complexities could never take place simply because the organism decided that it was desirable. Modern man is unable to do this by merely exercising his thought processes, and such deliberately decided development certainly was not possible for life forms that are extremely elementary when compared with modern man.

## Breeding Experiments with Humans

QUESTION: Do you believe that visitors from space actually did conduct breeding experiments with humans?

ANSWER: I do not, but Von Daniken certainly argues for that theory. He states, "The gods of the dim past have left countless traces which we can read and decipher today for the first time . . . space travel, so topical today, was not a problem, but a reality, to the men of thousands of years ago." [6] In statements such as this Von Daniken's theory is put forward as though it has become fact, with evidences that the gods left behind now able to be understood by modern men. Von Daniken goes on:

> Even though I do not yet know who these extra-terrestrial intelligences were or from which planet they came, I nevertheless proclaim that these "strangers" annihilated part of mankind existing at

the time and produced a new, perhaps the first, Homo sapiens.[7]

In that quotation he acknowledges he does not know where these extraterrestrial visitors came from, though later he speculates that they might have come from the constellation of the Pleiades or from Mars.[8]

QUESTION: Does Von Daniken state that these people actually lived on the earth?

ANSWER: He speculates that if they were Martian men they would have been bigger than Earth men because of the difference in gravity. He further speculates that these were beings "who could move enormous blocks of stone, who instructed men in arts still unknown on earth, and who finally died out." [9]

## Sons of God and Daughters of Men

QUESTION: What do you make of the Bible verse that the sons of God saw the daughters of men that they were fair, that they took wives from among them, and that there were giants in the earth—does not that mean there were breeding experiments by extraterrestrial visitors who had sex relations with women on earth? [10]

ANSWER: There are those who believe that this verse refers to fallen angelic beings lusting after human flesh, having sex relations with women, and giants being the result of the union. Others point out that the term "took them wives" is the normal expression used both in the Bible and throughout the East for the marriage relationship, and does not refer to a casual sex act.

Those who reject the interpretation that the verse is referring to fallen angels argue that the godly line of Seth took wives from the ungodly line of Cain. They point out that the expression, "There were giants in the earth in those days," does not necessarily follow as a causal relationship of what had gone before. It could simply be a statement of fact —men were much nearer to creation and to perfection, and this on its own could account for the fact that there were giants in the earth. Christian scholars are divided on the issue. Some are emphatic that the verse refers to fallen angels having relations with women, and others are just as emphatic that it refers to the two lines of human beings coming together. Certainly the Bible does not endorse the breeding experiments to which Von Daniken points.

## Enoch and Elijah Taken to Heaven

QUESTION: Was Enoch taken to heaven in a fiery chariot?

ANSWER: Von Daniken states that he was, but the Bible simply says, "And Enoch walked with God: and he was not; for God took him" (Genesis 5:24). The Bible does not refer to a fiery heavenly chariot, as Von Daniken does, and it seems he is confusing the biblical record with a Jewish legend about Enoch —an imaginative extension of the biblical incident. Possibly, however, Von Daniken was confusing Enoch with the prophet Elijah, for the Bible does state that Elisha saw Elijah going into heaven in a chariot of horses and fire. If we are to accept that this literally was a chariot, then we must surely believe that there were horses also galloping into the sky—obviously there is a measure of symbolism in the biblical record. The use of such figurative language does not detract from the literal happening of a man being transferred from earth to heaven.

## An Atomic Blast at Sodom?

QUESTION: Do you believe that the ancient cities of Sodom and Gomorrah were destroyed by an atomic explosion?

ANSWER: No. The evidence of the destruction of these

two cities comes from the Bible, and it does not speak of an atomic explosion. In 1924 an expedition under Professor Mervyn Kyle found evidence of a walled area at Bab-Edh Dra'a in the Moabite foothills—it had been built and occupied by the Canaanites until about the time of Abraham. Then it was deserted for several centuries. Very recently four other sites have been identified on the east side of the Dead Sea, and the evidence points to occupation at the time of Abraham. It seems highly probable that these are the ruins of the five cities of the plain that were involved in this biblical incident.

QUESTION: Briefly, what do you think happened to cause the destruction of those two cities?

ANSWER: Various scientific experts have combined to give a reconstruction: it seems that an earthquake ground up rocks that were at the edge of the geological fault which is known to run right through that area. Then the natural gases from the oilfield beneath the southern part of the Dead Sea ignited, forcing the layers of the earth to be hurled into the air, and consequently rocks, sulfur, bitumen, and salt were all literally rained from the sky. Lot's wife was apparently enclosed in rock salt. High up on nearby Jebel Usdum, Arabic for Mount Sodom, the marl gives evidence of the earth's strata brought together as by intense heat. Great quantities of bitumen are still there, high up the mountainside.

QUESTION: Does not the Bible record imply an atomic blast?

ANSWER: No, though the Bible record does give one very delightful piece of local color concerning the pressure involved in the destruction. At Genesis 19: 28 we read that Abraham looked and saw the smoke ascending as the smoke of a furnace. He was at Hebron, and there were mountain ridges between where he stood and the destruction itself. He could not have seen the fire, but he could see the smoke that had billowed high into the sky.

QUESTION: So heavenly visitors did not set off an atomic blast, as Erich Von Daniken implied?

ANSWER: To suggest that the heavenly visitors had come from a spaceship and had set off an atomic blast is adding very greatly to the record as it is in the Bible—there is no such implication. It appears that the forces of nature were utilized to bring about the Divine purposes at the appropriate time.

## The Egyptians and Their Chariots—and that "Elephant" Island

QUESTION: Von Daniken speaks of Egyptian Pharaohs appearing in gleaming heavenly chariots—can you comment? [11]

ANSWER: The particular statement which Von Daniken quotes relates to the god Ptah. He was actually a manifestation of the sun god Ra, in association with the ancient Egyptian city of Memphis. Ra the sun god traversed the sky daily. The living Pharaoh was the present manifestation of Ra, and when that Pharaoh died, he was reabsorbed back into Ra. By this belief, in a sense the departed Pharaoh now made daily journeys in the sun—the gleaming heavenly chariot. There are many writings in Egypt and elsewhere which speak symbolically of the journeys of the sun, and the Egyptians regarded the Pharaoh as the manifestation of that great power. This was the way the ancient Egyptians explained the personal manifestation of the impersonal power that apparently controlled the skies.

QUESTION: Erich Von Daniken speaks about Elephantine Island in the Nile River being in the shape of an elephant when photographed from a great height. Can you comment?

ANSWER: Von Daniken states that even in the older

texts this island was called "Elephantine" because it always resembled an elephant. He then goes on to ask, "How did the ancient Egyptians know that, because this shape can only be recognized from an airplane at a great height?" [12]

Actually the word *"elephantinos"* does not mean "elephant," but "ivory"—it is a translation of the Egyptian word *"Yeb,"* and the island was already known as Yeb before the times of the Greeks who called it "Elephantine." In any case, the island does not resemble the shape of an elephant today, as is implied in *Chariots of the Gods?* Even if it did, this could well argue more against Von Daniken's argument than for it, for relatively small river islands tend to change their shape over long periods of time.

## That Electrified Ark

QUESTION: Erich Von Daniken suggests that the Ark of the Covenant was electrified. Do you agree?

ANSWER: Let me quote what Erich Von Daniken says:

Without actually consulting Exodus, I seem to remember that the Ark was often surrounded by flashing sparks and that Moses made use of this "transmitter" whenever he needed help and advice.[13]

You may consult Exodus from cover to cover but you will find no mention of those supposed flashing sparks. This concept of electricity associated with the Ark is not according to the facts given in the Bible. Nor do we read that the priests wore special protective clothing. In the Bible we learn that Uzzah put out his hand and touched the Ark. He met the judgment of God for intruding into an area associated with worship, an area which was sacred to the priests alone. There is nothing whatever in the Bible to suggest that he was electrocuted. Nor do we read anything about "alloys," as Von Daniken claims. The Bible mentions only pure gold.

QUESTION: Could that Ark of the Covenant have been electrically charged?

ANSWER: This is dealt with in some detail in *Crash Go the Chariots*. The Ark was completely covered inside and out with gold, and it could not have been electrically charged. Nor could one of the cherubim figures above the Ark have been used as a microphone, as Von Daniken suggests, for the Bible makes it clear at Exodus 25:22 that God communed with Moses from *between* the cherubim *above* the Mercy Seat. In addition, it is clear that God talked to Moses and Moses talked to God *before* the Ark was constructed.

QUESTION: Is it a fact that a university constructed a copy of the Ark of the Covenant, following the instructions given in the Bible, and that it proved to be electrically dangerous?

ANSWER: Erich Von Daniken's answers to this question have been more than vague. No such university project is known, and the supposed university has denied all knowledge of this project. In fact, would a university really be prepared to use the great amount of gold required for a project of this nature? This theory about the Ark being electrically charged has not stood investigation.

## Ezekiel's Vision and Space Vehicles

QUESTION: According to Erich Von Daniken, the vehicle that Ezekiel saw and described in the first chapter of his prophecy was a space chariot, and he says that the gods took Ezekiel with them in their vehicle. Do you agree?

ANSWER: Erich Von Daniken himself goes on to say that "this kind of locomotion seems to me to be quite incompatible with the idea of an Almighty God." [14]

In that same chapter Ezekiel says this was a vision, and none of the other captives with him saw the vision. Obviously no other explanation is needed, for Ezekiel is himself making it clear that it was not a literal vehicle.

QUESTION: Is there any other evidence from within the Bible that what Ezekiel saw was a vision?

ANSWER: Ezekiel uses language that makes it clear he is talking about visions. He even refers to himself as a sign (Ezekiel 12:11)—he is a living symbol, testifying to the future exile of his own people. He uses language such as that the heavens were opened (Ezekiel 1:1), and he says that the hand of the Lord was upon him.

In that same chapter where the so-called vehicle is described, he also talks of God being set on a great throne *above* that vehicle (Ezekiel 1:26), not confined within it. God is depicted in human form, sitting on a throne, just as a human king would sit. It is what is called anthropomorphic language—describing God in human terms.

Even the "four living creatures" associated with that "chariot" are tied into a form of symbolism then common, for somewhat similar figures were constructed by Babylonians, Assyrians, and other people of that time.

Ezekiel is able to describe what is taking place in Jerusalem hundreds of miles away (Ezekiel 8:3); then, in the next chapter, he gives details about the fall of Jerusalem, long before it actually happened. He talks about a valley full of dry bones, and he watches as those bones come together, flesh and sinew come upon them, and life returns. This is a vision of Israel coming together again as a living nation.

This vision of the so-called vehicle took place in the middle of a great refugee camp. It was a densely

packed area, yet nobody but Ezekiel saw this thing—
saw it within his own mind. Clearly it was not a
spaceship that came zooming down out of the sky.

## Could Ezekiel's Vehicle Be Built Today?

QUESTION: It has been claimed that a vehicle like the
one Ezekiel saw has been reconstructed, and that
such a vehicle is possible physically. Do you agree?

ANSWER: The vehicle that Ezekiel saw in his vision
moved in all directions at once. If a vehicle was
built, having four separate moving components that
went in all directions, they could only go as far as
the physical limits of the machine itself would allow.
Then they would either change direction or would
necessarily break away from the other moving parts.

By this vision Ezekiel was being shown symbolically that almighty God cannot be confined in space
or time as mortals are confined.

QUESTION: Have you read that an engineer who helped
develop the Skylab Space Shuttle and the Saturn 5
Rocket has become convinced that Ezekiel was describing an actual vehicle, and that this engineer has
come up with drawings of what such a craft would
look like?

ANSWER: Yes, I have read that report of Josef Blum-
rich, and I have seen copies of the drawings. It looks
like a flying saucer, but in addition—as I would describe it—it has four helicopter-type vehicles protruding out and down from the sides of the main
body. If we were to accept that Ezekiel is describing
a literal vehicle and not simply a vision, we would
also have to accept the rest of Ezekiel's description,
including his statement that the beings went straight
forward without turning as they went.

Verse 16 of Ezekiel, chapter 1, says that the construction was as though it was a wheel inside another
wheel. We read on and find that when the beings

moved, they went in any of their four directions without turning as they went. The whole description in Ezekiel, chapter 1, is hardly that of four different machines attached to one central body. Laws of physics would demand that within a very limited space those four vehicles, if they continued going off in any direction they wanted, would become disconnected. They would separate from the main body and from each other. As we have already stated, Ezekiel himself says this was a vision—a vision not seen by others who were with him at the time.

## The Dead Sea Scrolls

QUESTION: Is Erich Von Daniken accurate when he writes about the Dead Sea Scrolls?

ANSWER: He refers to "the Apocalypse of Moses" as being among hitherto unknown texts recovered with the Dead Sea Scrolls. That particular text has been known for many centuries and was typical of Jewish writings put out about the time of the New Testament. Bible scholars do not regard that Apocalypse as genuinely coming from Moses.

Von Daniken is unreliable at other points also about the Dead Sea Scrolls, as when he talks about "the astonishing information" in the so-called Book of Enoch relating to Noah and the coming flood. The actual compilation of this book dates to approximately New Testament times, though some of the material it contains is from a much earlier time. However, as with "the Apocalypse of Moses," this book has been known for many centuries, quite independently of the Dead Sea Scrolls.

Those Scrolls do not give us "new information" that was supposedly given to Noah, and Von Daniken does not produce new evidence at this point.

## The Pillar that Does Not Rust

QUESTION: Can you comment on the Indian iron pillar that Erich Von Daniken says has been standing for thousands of years and does not rust?

ANSWER: That pillar is situated at Delhi in India, and its story is well known. Many people regard it as a lucky charm, but it is not entirely rustproof, and, despite his statement to the contrary, it does contain some phosphorus. It shows some signs of rust, though it is remarkably well preserved. There is similar metal in New Jersey, U.S.A., known as "bob iron." It certainly did not come from astronauts or from outer space. It is strange that these astronauts never brought any of their new metals with them—they made the poor human slaves work with ordinary metals, stone, and wood that are native to the lowly planet Earth!

## Piri Re'is and His Remarkable Map

QUESTION: Who was the Turkish sailor Piri Re'is, and where did he get the information for his remarkable map?

ANSWER: The word Re'is means "admiral," and Piri Re'is was formerly a pirate who was offered amnesty and became a highly effective Turkish admiral.

According to Von Daniken, this was part of a map of the world taken from a very great height, and he claims it proved to be virtually identical with another map taken from a spaceship as it was over Cairo. Actually considerable juggling is needed to make the two maps appear to be similar, and the Piri Re'is map contains a number of errors—such as the Amazon River appearing twice.

Piri Re'is himself stated on the famous map that he made use of twenty different earlier maps as he prepared his work, and he stated also that he had consulted a sailor who sailed with the famous Colombo —Columbus had "discovered" the North American continent just a few years before this map was issued.

This matter of the Piri Re'is map is dealt with admirably by my former colleague at the Australian Institute of Archaeology, Reverend Gordon Garner:

> The map in question was found in the Imperial Palace at Constantinople and is dated to the year A.D. 1513 (Moslem year 919). Admiral Piri claims on the parchment to have used twenty different charts as the basis of his map. These range from Alexander the Great's time to Columbus and four Portuguese navigators—hardly a copy of one ancient map!
>
> Hapgood tries to establish that the original was drawn during the Ice Age, not before it as Von Daniken implies (referring to a period of over 600,000 years ago). To do so he has to explain away some of the "corruptions" introduced by the Alexandrian geographers! These include 900 miles of coastland missing from the South American east coast (38½° to 47° south), the Amazon River drawn twice (a duplication undoubtedly due to Piri using several small sections), the Caribbean section 78¾° out of alignment with the rest of the map and, what is obvious to even the untrained eye, the Antarctic joined directly to South America, thus ignoring 600 miles of ocean. Madeira and the Falkland Islands are both out of their correct locations, even after Hapgood has made allowance for various errors.[15]

## A Common Mistake about the Antarctic

These points are devastating to Von Daniken's hypothesis concerning the Piri Re'is map. The Turkish admiral did a fine piece of work considering the limitations of his times—it is another example of the splendid achievements of the Renaissance period. Nevertheless, the map was certainly not photographed from the air, as Von Daniken would have us believe.

Reverend Garner further comments:

It is interesting to note that Hapgood, in dealing with the wrong location of the Antarctic, acknowledges that this is a common mistake "in all the maps of the Renaissance" showing this continent. This surely points to a cartographical error of that age rather than of the past. That they were confused is clear, as what is allegedly Queen Maud Land is stated on Piri's map to be very hot and abounding with snakes!

Finally, the whole projection is in error because, according to Hapgood, the earth is assumed to be 4½ percent larger than it actually is. This error Hapgood attributes to the Alexandrian geographers who followed the estimate of the Greek, Eratosthenes.

Mr. Garner shows that the admiral himself had already rejected Von Daniken's hypothesis, even before it was written. Mr. Garner states:

One may follow Hapgood—though Von Daniken does not do this—and try to restore the map to a reasonable representation. But one thing is clear, the map is not "absolutely" and "fantastically accurate." If it is a copy of copies, it has been so corrupted that any space photograph with its alleged distortion has been completely lost. Surely the Turkish admiral is to be believed in preference: he compiled his chart from various maps of small areas.

The chariots still crash in the mists emerging from Von Daniken's own mind.

## When Was Venus Formed?

QUESTION: Do you agree with Von Daniken as to when the planet Venus was formed?

ANSWER: Von Daniken appears to be somewhat confused on this matter. He refers to the viewpoint of Dr. Emanuel Velikovsky who put forward a theory about Venus in *Worlds in Collision*. Velikovsky associated the formation of Venus with the action that caused many strange happenings of the past, including the opening of the Red Sea when the Israelites were fleeing from Egypt in the days of Moses. Elsewhere in his book, Von Daniken states there is a cave drawing "in the mountainous Asian region of Kohistan . . . (that) reproduces the exact position of the constellations as they actually were 10,000 years ago. Venus and the earth are joined by lines." [16] Obviously both statements cannot be correct—if Venus was formed less than 4,000 years ago when Moses led the children of Israel out of Egypt, it certainly could not have been formed 10,000 years ago as well.

## Life on Other Planets?

QUESTION: Erich Von Daniken says that there is no doubt that there are other planets similar to the earth. What do you think?

ANSWER: The very document to which Von Daniken refers to show that there is no doubt about the existence of planets with atmospheric and other conditions similar to the earth's includes this statement: "Estimation of the average number of planets per system with environments suitable for the development of life is a matter of pure guesswork." [17]

QUESTION: Could you outline briefly what you see as the problems associated with intelligent life on other planets?

ANSWER: This was done for us by the late Professor Frederick H. Giles, Jr., in an appendix to *Crash Go the Chariots*. According to Dr. Giles, "The first problem is, 'Are there other planets anyway?' Then if there is even one such planet, will it have the right conditions for the maintaining of life—such conditions as the right temperature range. For example, if the temperature is too high, the complexity of the chemical processes is such that they simply do not hold together. If the temperature is too low, the chemical processes do not occur rapidly enough for living things to arrive at a point of change, and therefore even the process of thinking would be out of the question. So it follows that if we are thinking of a form of life that involves chemistry, the temperature range is very important. And there are other problems: such a planet must be commodious—it must not be too heavy or it would plaster life to its earth; it must not be too light, for some sort of atmosphere would need to be maintained. Then, too, the conjectured planet must be the right distance from the star it spun off, and also there needs to be a fantastically long period of time for the emergence of a self-replicating system."

Dr. Giles then makes it clear that he is not necessarily talking about intelligent life but simply "life." He states that "the emergence of sentient, conscious, intelligent life involves further problems. If all the other conditions were met—all the problems we have already discussed—we would still need enough time for the complexity of intelligent life to appear. And even if there were intelligent beings, that does not necessarily mean that their technology would be highly developed. It would be an exceedingly complex operation for them to communicate with beings on earth or any other planet—even if they had the tremendous periods of time necessary for such an operation. Even at a conservative estimate it would take four light-years for such a signal to be sent and received on earth, and then four more light-years for the return signal. By that time the original operators would have been long since dead."

To summarize, I cannot say there is no life on other planets but I can say that it is wrong to state, as Von Daniken states, that "there is no doubt" about the existence of other planets with the necessary conditions for the maintenance of life such as there is on the planet Earth. This is the only planet about which we have definite knowledge.

## Yet Another "Secret" Source Book

QUESTION: Are Von Daniken's later books any more acceptable than *Chariots of the Gods?*

ANSWER: I have before me a report by Gavin Sauter in Australia's highly reputable *Sydney Morning Herald*, dated March 24, 1973. It is the report of an extensive interview with Erich Von Daniken and he discusses each of Von Daniken's books. He mentions that in his second book, *Return to the Stars* (later called *Gods from Outer Space*), Von Daniken quotes at length from *The Book of Dzyan* which is supposed to tell all about the ancient world, creation, and the evolution of mankind over millions of years. In *Gods from Outer Space* Von Daniken states that this book originated beyond the Himalayas.[18] He was asked where a copy could be found, and referred to *The Secret Doctrine* by the Russian theosophist Madame H. P. Blavatsky, dating to 1888. In her introduction to that work, Madame Blavatsky makes this admission:

> *The Book of Dzyan* is utterly unknown to our philologists, or at any rate was never heard of by them under its present name. This is, of course, a great drawback to those who follow the methods

of research prescribed by official science; but to the students of occultism, and to every genuine occultist, this will be of little moment.

It may be of little moment to students of occultism, but it is indeed a problem to those who undertake research at an academic level.

Gavin Sauter further analyzes Von Daniken's writings, and offers the same sort of criticism concerning each of Von Daniken's books.

## Man in the Space Age

QUESTION: Is Von Daniken taken as seriously as he was when his books first appeared on the market?

ANSWER: In my opinion he is not. Many people now know that his writings are unreliable, and even some of those who applaud him believe that he has gone too far—for example, in his criticisms of archaeologists and the science of archaeology itself. He is not taken entirely seriously as a writer by many, though there are still thousands who believe in him as though he were a great new prophet of truth.

Von Daniken's books hit the market at more or less the same time that Neil Armstrong first walked on the moon. Man was not necessarily limited to earth after all—despite all the equipment and paraphernalia that was necessary, that giant step was taken, and man really is in the space age. Now we are more used to the idea, but mankind is still wondering. Perhaps there is something out there . . . watching . . . ready. . . .

In addition, Von Daniken touches on the subject of UFOs. He himself has stated that when he talks about visitors from outer space, he is not dealing with UFOs. The matter of UFOs that are apparently appearing in our skies at the present time is a different subject. However, the fact of their activity has increased interest in his hypotheses.

It is relevant to state that in this book we have not attempted to debunk the concept of the UFOs as such: indeed, in my book *UFOs and Their Mission Impossible* I make it very clear that I fully accept that there really are UFOs—and give documented evidence that demonstrates evil overtones associated with that phenomenon. Since the publication of the Condon Report in 1969, scientists have been forced to take seriously the possibility of paraphysical activity being involved with UFOs. Paraphysical activity involves the same sort of phenomena as with séances and such things. The investigation was funded by the United States government, and was headed up by a top physicist, Dr. E. U. Condon of Colorado University.

## Conjectures, Way-Out Theories, and Foregone Conclusions

QUESTION: How would you summarize the conjectures of Erich Von Daniken?

ANSWER: This also was very well done by Dr. Giles. He stated: "He takes conjectures, accepts them as facts, builds on to them way-out theories, and presents his 'many small coincidences' according to his own preconceived notions. He deliberately chooses the unconnected, weaves a semblance of connection around it, and puts his theories out as foregone conclusions. This approach is often used by writers, and it may make exciting reading, but one dare not accept it as substantially credible."

QUESTION: You do not take Von Daniken's conclusions seriously?

ANSWER: Many of his hypotheses cannot be substantiated. He tends to distort facts according to his own preconceived notions. He belittles scholarship when that scholarship is opposed to his own hypotheses—this is especially so in the field of archaeology. He carries his readers along by flattering them with a "We know better" approach. Evidence opposing his viewpoint is brushed lightly aside. He confuses chronological and geographical data. He seems relatively unaware of the great technological achievements of men who lived thousands of years ago—by his hypothesis, the only really satisfactory explanation for those achievements is that astronauts intervened in the affairs of men.

## Von Daniken's Success as a Writer

QUESTION: How do you explain Erich Von Daniken's success as a writer?

ANSWER: He has sensed the human urge for an explanation "from beyond"—he has shown very real "psychological" discernment and commercial acumen. He reaches masses of people by his superficially exciting explanations, especially by his insistence on other-worldly visitors. Man is so created that he has a desire to find that which is beyond—a God or "gods" whose power is greater than that of man himself. For the one who rejects the true God, Von Daniken's superficially exciting theories at first sight appear to answer questions satisfactorily. He offers a plausible—but ultimately unconvincing—alternative. Something similar can be seen with the Israelites' turning to Baal when they did not want to accept the holy standards of Yahweh.

It is perhaps significant that each of his three titles relates to God or Divine involvement. We have seen also that he has a very great interest in life's origins. However, his highly provocative viewpoints are hardly acceptable to those who expect a reasoned basis before a theory can be considered seriously.

The fact is, his chariots still crash.

# NOTES

*Chapter 1*

1. *Encounter*, August, 1973, p. 12.
2. *The Gold of the Gods*, Erich Von Daniken, p. 21.
3. *Encounter*, August, 1973, p. 12.
4. *Ibid.*, p. 8.
5. *Ibid.*, p. 12.
6. *Ibid.*, p. 12.
7. Von Daniken, *op. cit.*, p. 1.
8. *Ibid.*, p. 5.
9. *Encounter*, August, 1973, pp. 9, 10.
10. Von Daniken, *op. cit.*, p. 6.
11. *Ibid.*, p. 7.
12. *Ibid.*, p. 8.
13. *Ibid.*, p. 8.
14. *Ibid.*, p. 9.
15. *Ibid.*, p. 11.
16. *Ibid.*, p. 9.
17. The Detroit *Free Press*. Similar reports have been made to this author.
18. Von Daniken, *op. cit.*, p. 17.
19. *Ibid.*, p. 19.
20. *Ibid.*, p. 19.
21. *Ibid.*, p. 28.
22. *Encounter*, August, 1973, p. 17.
23. Von Daniken, *op. cit.*, p. 37.
24. *Encounter*, August, 1973, p. 13.
25. *Ibid.*, p. 13.
26. Von Daniken, *op. cit.*, pp. 9, 10.
27. *Ibid.*, p. 10.

28. *Encounter*, August, 1973, p. 12.
29. *Ibid.*, p. 17.
30. *Ibid.*, p. 12.
31. *Ibid.*, pp. 9, 10.


Chapter 2

1. *Chariots of the Gods?*, Erich Von Daniken, p. 74.
2. *Recent Discoveries in Bible Lands*, W. F. Albright, pp. 70ff.
3. *Citadels of Mystery*, L. Sprague de Camp and Catherine C. de Camp, p. 41.
4. *Mysteries from Forgotten Worlds*, Charles Berlitz, p. 66.
5. *Ibid.*, p. 67.
6. Von Daniken, *op. cit.*, p. 78.
7. de Camp, *op. cit.*, p. 31.
8. Von Daniken, *op. cit.*, p. 79.
9. *Ibid.*, p. 79.
10. *Ibid.*, p. 79.
11. *Ibid.*, p. 75.
12. *Ancient Near Eastern Texts*, Professor J. Pritchard, p. 227.
13. Von Daniken, *op. cit.*, p. 80.
14. *Ibid.*, pp. 80, 81.
15. *Ibid.*, p. 81.
16. *Ibid.*, p. 82.
17. *Ibid.*, p. 83.
18. *Ibid.*, pp. 83, 84.
19. Berlitz, *op. cit.*, p. 68.

Chapter 3

1. *Mysteries from Forgotten Worlds*, Charles Berlitz, p. 128.
2. *Yahweh and the Gods of Canaan*, W. F. Albright, p. 87.
3. *Tells, Tombs and Treasures*, Robert T. Boyd.
4. Berlitz, *op. cit.*, p. 129.
5. *Citadels of Mystery*, L. Sprague de Camp and Catherine C. de Camp, pp. 243-4.
6. Berlitz, *op. cit.*, pp. 181-2.
7. *Ibid.*, pp. 186-7.
8. *Ibid.*, p. 189.
9. *Chariots of the Gods?*, Erich Von Daniken, p. 91.
10. *Ibid.*, p. 91.
11. *Gods from Outer Space*, Erich Von Daniken, pp. 116f.
12. *Ibid.*, p. 116.
13. *Ibid.*, p. 117.
14. *Ibid.*, p. 116.
15. Von Daniken, *Chariots of the Gods?*, p. 91.
16. Von Daniken, *Gods from Outer Space*, p. 118.
17. *Ibid.*, p. 64.

Chapter 4

1. *Gods from Outer Space*, Erich Von Daniken, p. 40.
2. *Ibid.*, p. 40.
3. *Ibid.*, p. 111; *Chariots of the Gods?*, p. 26, etc.
4. Sacramento Creation Science Society leaflet *Creation or Evolution? a Christian view of science*, p. 11.
5. "Time, Life and History in the Light of 15,000

Radio Carbon Dates," *The Creation Research Society Quarterly,* June, 1970, p. 56.

6. *Ibid.*, p. 59.

7. *Yahweh and the Gods of Canaan,* Athlone Press, London, 1968, p. 86.

8. *Tells, Tombs and Treasures,* Robert T. Boyd, p. 72.

9. *Carbon 14 and Other Radio-Active Dating Methods,* Dr. George Howe, p. 11.

10. *The Flood and the Fossils,* George Mulfinger, pp. 4, 5, 14, 15.

11. *The Creation Research Society Quarterly, op. cit.,* p. 7.

12. I.C.R. Impact Series No. 8, p. 14.

13. *The Gold of the Gods,* Erich Von Daniken, p. 178.

14. *Journal of Geophysical Research,* Vol. 73/14, July 15, 1968.

15. "Dating of the Moon Rocks," Duane T. Gish, Ph.D., in *Creation Science Report* Vol. 1, No. 2., March/April, 1972.

16. *The Age of the Earth,* L. Hallonquist, pp. 4, 5.

17. *Radio-Active Dating,* L. Hallonquist, p. 2.

18. Dr. George Howe, *op. cit.,* p. 12.

19. *Science Journal,* November, 1968.

20. I.C.R. Impact Series No. 11, p. 2.

21. *The Mystery Tracks in Dinosaur Valley,* Stanley E. Taylor, "Films for Christ," Peoria, Illinois.

22. *Evolution or Creation?,* Professor H. Enoch, p. 132f.

23. Sacramento Creation Science Society leaflet, *op. cit.,* p. 10.

24. Dr. George Howe, *op. cit.,* p. 9.

25. Elaborated in *In the Beginning, God,* Clifford Wilson, p. 33.

26. Dr. George Howe, *op. cit.,* p. 8.

## Chapter 5

1. *Chariots of the Gods?*, Erich Von Daniken, p. 94.
2. *Ibid.*, p. 94.
3. *Mysteries from Forgotten Worlds*, Charles Berlitz.
4. *Ibid.*, p. 86.
5. *Ibid.*, p. 83.
6. *Citadels of Mystery*, L. Sprague de Camp and Catherine C. de Camp, p. 64.
7. *Ibid.*, p. 56.
8. *Ibid.*, p. 57.
9. *Chariots of the Gods?*, Erich Von Daniken, p. 94.

## Chapter 6

1. *Archaeology Made Simple*, Rhoda A. Hendricks, pp. 168ff.
2. *Chariots of the Gods?*, Erich Von Daniken, p. 103.
3. *Ibid.*, p. 103.
4. *Some Trust in Chariots,* Ed. E. W. Castle and B. B. Thiering, p. 54.
5. Von Daniken, *op. cit.*, pp. 55, 56.
6. *Ibid.*, p. 99.
7. *Ibid.*, p. 99.
8. *Ibid.*, p. 101.
9. Castle and Thiering, *op. cit.*, p. 53.
10. Von Daniken, *op. cit.*, p. 99.
11. *Ibid.*, p. 99.

12. *Ibid.*, p. 100.
13. Castle and Thiering, *op. cit.*, **p. 16.**
14. *Ibid*, p. 51.
15. *Ibid.*, p. 55.
16. Von Daniken, *op. cit.*, p. 23.
17. *Ibid.*, p. 69.
18. *Ibid.*, pp. 27, 28.
19. *Ibid.*, p. 93.
20. *Ibid.*, p. 100.
21. *Ibid.*, p. 101.
22. *Ibid.*, p. 100.

*Chapter 7*

1. *Chariots of the Gods?*, Erich Von Daniken, p. 17.
2. *In Search of Ancient Mysteries*, Alan and Sally Landsburg, pp. 65-66.

*Chapter 8*

1. *Gods from Outer Space*, Erich Von Daniken, e.g. pp. 61ff.
2. Some of the details of these and other epics are taken from my earlier volume *That Incredible Book . . . the Bible*. They are now included because of their relevance for the present survey.
3. *Documents from Old Testament Times*, D. Winton Thomas, p. 12.
4. A. R. Millard, in the Tyndale Biblical Archaeology Lecture for 1966.
5. *Ancient Orient and Old Testament*, K. A. Kitchen, p. 89.

176              *Clifford Wilson*

6. *Middle Eastern Mythology*, F. H. Hook, p. 114.
7. *Illustrations from Biblical Archaeology*, D. J. Wiseman, p. 9.
8. Winton Thomas, *op. cit.*, p. 23.
9. *Chariots of the Gods?*, Erich Von Daniken, p. 45.
10. *Ibid.*, p. 49.
11. *Ibid.*, p. 49.
12. Winton Thomas, *op. cit.*, p. 22.
13. Von Daniken, *op. cit.*, pp. 48-49.
14. *Ibid.*, p. 49 (paras. 2 and 4).
15. *Ibid.*, p. 62.
16. Examples include:

    Genesis 1:1 —*God created the heavens and the earth* (cf. 2:4).
    Genesis 2:4 —*When they were created* (cf. 5:2).
    Genesis 6:10—*Shem, Ham and Japheth* (cf. 10:1).
    Genesis 10:1 —*After the flood* (cf. 11:10).
    Genesis 11:26—*Abram, Nahor and Haran* (cf. 11:27).
    Genesis 25:12—*Abraham's son* (cf. 25:19);
    Genesis 36:1 —*Who is Edom* (cf. 36:8).
    Genesis 36:9 —*Father of the Edomites* (literally "Father Edom") (cf. 36:43).

17. *Yahweh and the Gods of Canaan*, W. F. Albright, p. 86.
18. Anchor Bible, "Genesis," pp. 74-76.
19. Selected from *That Incredible Book . . . the Bible*, Clifford Wilson, pp. 37ff.
20. *Ibid.*, p. 39.
21. *Yahweh and the Gods of Canaan*, W. F. Albright, p. 87.
22. *Tells, Tombs and Treasures*, Robert T. Boyd.
23. *Biblical Archaeology*, p. 45.

Chapter 9

1. *Encounter,* August, 1973, p. 15.
2. *Ibid.,* p. 11.
3. *Ibid.,* p. 15.
4. *Unsolved Mysteries of the Past,* Otto Binder, p. 121.
5. *Ibid.,* p. 121.
6. *Chariots of the Gods?,* Erich Von Daniken, Introduction, p. viii.
7. *Ibid.,* Introduction, p. viii.
8. *Ibid.,* pp. 56, 62, 129, etc.
9. *Ibid.,* p. 45.
10. Genesis 6:2.
11. Von Daniken, *op. cit.,* p. 63.
12. *Ibid.,* p. 63.
13. *Ibid.,* pp. 40f.
14. *Ibid.,* p. 40.
15. *Chariots of the Gods?—A Critical Review* (2nd ed.), p. 17.
16. Von Daniken, *Chariots of the Gods?,* p. 27.
17. *Extraterrestrial Intelligent Life and Interstellar Communication:* An Informal Discussion, J. P. T. Pearman, p. 289.
18. *Gods from Outer Space,* Erich Von Daniken, p. 137.

In addition to Erich Von Daniken's three books (*Chariots of the Gods?*, *Gods From Outer Space*—also published as *Return to the Stars,* and *The Gold of the Gods*) a number of pamphlets, booklets, and journal articles have been consulted. These are listed at the appropriate points throughout the text, and are included in the notes to the chapters. The following are the more substantial books referred to in the preparation of *Crash Go the Chariots* and the present *The Chariots Still Crash.*

ACTS & FACTS, Institute for Creation Research, San Diego. Helpful in relation to carbon dating and allied subjects.

ALBRIGHT, W. F. *Recent Discoveries in Bible Lands.* Funk & Wagnalls Co., New York, 1936.

ALBRIGHT, W. F. *Yahweh and the Gods of Canaan. An Historical Analysis of Two Contrasting Faiths.* Athlone Press, University of London, 1968.

ALBRIGHT, W. F. "Archaeological Discovery and the Scriptures," *Christianity Today,* Vol. XII, Number 19, June 1968.

ALBRIGHT, William Foxwell. *From the Stone Age to Christianity.* First published in 1940 by The Johns Hopkins Press, Baltimore. Re-issued revised by Doubleday Anchor Books 1946 and 1957.

ALBRIGHT, William Foxwell, *The Biblical Period from Abraham to Ezra.* Harper & Row, New York. Revised and Expanded Edition, 1963.

BARNETT, R. D. *Illustrations of Old Testament History.* British Museum Publication, 1968.

BEASLEY, W. J. *The Amazing Story of Sodom.* Gospel Literature Service, Bombay, 1957.

BERLITZ, Charles. *Mysteries from Forgotten Worlds.* Doubleday & Co., New York, 1972.

BOYD, R. T. *Tells, Tombs and Treasures. A Pictorial Guide to Biblical Archaeology.* Baker Book House, Grand Rapids, Michigan, 1950.

BOUQUET, A. C. *Sacred Books of the World.* Penguin, London, 1954.

BURIED HISTORY—Quarterly Journal of the Australian Institute of Archaeology, Melbourne.

CAMERON, A. G. W. (Ed.), *Report on Extraterrestrial Intelligent Life and Interstellar Communications: An Informal Discussion.* Institute for Space Studies, Goddard Space-Flight Center, NASA, published by W. A. Benjamin Inc.

CASTLE, E. W., and THIERING, B. B. (Eds.) *Some Trust in Chariots.* Westbooks Printing Ltd., Perth & Sydney, 1972.

CERAM, C. W. *A Picture History of Archaeology.* Thames and Hudson, London, 1963.

CHILDE, Gordon. *What Happened in History.* Pelican, London.

*CIVILIZATION PAST AND PRESENT*, volume 1, published by Scott, Foresman & Company, 1960.

De CAMP, L. S. and de CAMP, C. C. *Citadels of Mystery.* Fontana-Collins, London, 1972.

De PAOR, Liam. *Archaeology—an Illustrated Introduction.* Penguin.

EDWARDS, I. E. S. *The Pyramids of Egypt.* Penguin, Victoria, Australia, 1970.

ENCOUNTER, Melvin J. Lasky (Ed.). August 1973 Edition. Distributed by Gordon & Gotch, New York.

FAKHRY, Ahmed. *The Pyramids.* University of Chicago Press, Chicago, 1969.

FINEGAN, Jack. *Light from the Ancient Past.* Princeton University Press, New Jersey, 1959.

FREE, Joseph P. *Archaeology and Bible History*, 2nd ed. Wheaton, Ill., Scripture Press, 1950.

GANN, Thomas. *Maya Cities*. Duckworth, London, 1927.

GARNER, Gordon. *Chariots of the Gods—a Critical Review*. Aust. Institute of Archaeology, Melbourne, 1972.

GLUECK, Nelson. *Rivers in the Desert*. Philadelphia, Jewish Publication Society, 1959.

GOETZ, Delia and MORLEY, Sylvanus G. *Popol Vuh*. From the Spanish Translation by Adrian Recinos; University of Oklahoma Press, Norman, Oklahoma, 1950.

HEYERDAHL, Thor. *Aku-Aku—The Secret of Easter Island*. George Allen and Unwin Ltd., London, 1958.

HYERDAHL, Thor. *The Kon-Tiki Expedition*. George Allen and Unwin Ltd., London, 1950.

LEWIS, H. D., and SLATER, R. L. *The Study of Religions*, Pelican, 1966.

MORRIS, Henry M., GISH, Duane T., and HILLESTAD, George M. (Eds.) *Creation—Acts, Facts, Impacts*. ICR Publishing Co., San Diego, 1974.

PARROT, Andre. *The Tower of Babel*. New York Philosophical Library.

PFEIFFER, Charles F. *The Patriarchal Age*. Grand Rapids, Baker Book House, 1961.

PRITCHARD, James B. (Ed.), *Ancient Near East in Pictures Relating to the Old Testament*. Princeton, Princeton University Press, 1950.

PRITCHARD, J. B. *Ancient Near Eastern Texts Relating to the Old Testament*. Princeton University Press, New Jersey, 1955.

*PLAGUES OF EGYPT*. Reprint from *Buried History*. Aust. Institute of Archaeology, Melbourne.

SHAPLEY, Harlow. *Of Stars and Men*. Beacon Press, Boston, New York and Amsterdam, 1963.

SLUSHER, Harold S. *Critique of Radiometric Dating*. ICR Technical Monograph No. 2, San Diego, 1973.

THOMAS, D. W. *Documents from Old Testament Times*. Thomas Nelson & Sons Ltd., London, 1958.

THOMPSON, John Arthur. *The Bible and Archaeology*. Grand Rapids, Wm. B. Eerdmans Publishing Co., 1962.

THOMPSON, J. Eric S., *The Rise and Fall of Maya Civilization*. University of Oklahoma Press, Norman, Oklahoma, 1966.

UNGER, Merrill F. *Archaeology and the Old Testament*. Grand Rapids, Zondervan Publishing House, 1954.

*UNGER'S BIBLE DICTIONARY*, Moody Press, Chicago.

VON DANIKEN, Erich. *Chariots of the Gods?* Corgi Books, London, 1972.

VOS, Howard V. *Genesis and Archaeology*. Moody Press.

WILSON, Clifford. *Crash Go the Chariots*. Lancer Books Inc., New York, 1972.

WILSON, Clifford. *In the Beginning God . . .* Word of Truth Productions, Melbourne, 1970.

WILSON, Clifford. *Exploring the Old Testament*. Word of Truth Productions, Melbourne, 1970.

WILSON, Clifford. *That Incredible Book the Bible*. Word of Truth Productions, Melbourne, 1973.

WILSON, Clifford. *Archaeology and the Bible Student*. Aust. Institute of Archaeology, Melbourne, 1968.

WISEMAN, D. J. *Illustrations from Biblical Archaeology*. Grand Rapids, Wm. B. Eerdmans Publishing Co., 1958.

WISEMAN, P. J. *New Discoveries in Babylonia About Genesis*. Marshall, Morgan and Scott, London, 1946.

*Wycliffe Bible Commentary*. The Southwestern Company, Nashville, Tennessee, 1962.

# About the Author

Dr. Clifford Wilson is an Australian scholar who has traveled extensively. Married and the father of four children, he now resides in Victoria, Australia.

Dr. Wilson was the Director of the Australian Institute of Archaeology, and in that capacity served in 1969 as an Area Supervisor at the excavation of Gezer in Israel. He is a council member of the Commercial Education Society of Australia and in 1971 was honored as "An Outstanding Educator of America" while teaching at the University of South Carolina. Currently, he is Senior Lecturer in Education at the Monash University in Melbourne, being lecturer-in-charge of Psycholinguistics.

Among Dr. Wilson's previous books for NAL are *Crash Go the Chariots* and *UFOs and Their Mission Impossible.*

## Other SIGNET Titles You'll Want to Read

☐ **FOOTPRINTS ON THE SANDS OF TIME by L. M. Lewis.** The book that goes beyond **Chariots of the Gods?** to reveal the truth about the super race from the stars. Now, at last, the "Messengers from the Gods" are revealed as what they were —colonists from the stars, who, before they were brought to ruin, took man from the Stone Age and set him on the road to the stars. (#W6722—$1.50)

☐ **MYSTERY OF THE ANCIENTS: Early Spacemen and the Mayas by Eric and Craig Umland.** Virtually every question about the Mayas has been ignored by science for centuries— simply because there has seemed no rational solution to the puzzle this mysterious race has posed. Now at last we have the answers—in the most exciting, thought-provoking, and important book to ever change our whole way of looking at the past and present. (#W6511—$1.50)

☐ **THE ULTIMATE ELSEWHERE by J. H. Brennan.** There is an invisible world around you at this very moment! All over the world, people disappear in the blink of an eye, some never to be seen again, others to return with amazing stories of what they have seen and heard. Now at last a book moves through the centuries and around the globe to piece together the age-old mysteries that have haunted man since the beginning of time. . . . (#W6463—$1.50)

☐ **GODS AND SPACEMEN IN THE ANCIENT EAST by W. Raymond Drake.** Was there once a civilization on Earth that makes our present one seem like a kindergarten? Did its survivors remain to teach men the beginnings of wisdom while being worshipped by our primitive ancestors as supernatural beings? Not since **Chariots of the Gods?** have there been such sensational findings about the supermen from the stars! (#W5737—$1.50)

# HANDY FILES AND CASES FOR STORING MAGAZINES, CASSETTES, & 8-TRACK CARTRIDGES

### CASSETTE STORAGE CASES

Decorative cases, custom-made of heavy bookbinder's board, bound in Kid-Grain Leatherette, a gold-embossed design. Individual storage slots slightly tilted back to prevent handling spillage. Choice of: Black, brown, green.

#JC-30—30 unit size (13½x5½x6½")   $11.95 ea.
  3 for $33.00

#JC-60—60 unit size (13½x5½x12⅝")   $16.95 ea.
  3 for $48.00

### MAGAZINE VOLUME FILES

Keep your favorite magazines in mint condition. Heavy bookbinder's board is covered with scuff-resistant Kivar. Specify the title of the magazine and we'll send the right size case. If the title is well-known it will appear on the spine in gold letters. For society journals, a brass-rimmed window is attached and gold foil included—you type the title.

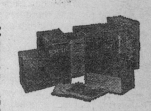

#J-MV—Magazine Volume Files   $4.95 ea.
  3 for $14.00
  6 for $24.00

### 8-TRACK CARTRIDGE STORAGE CASE

This attractive unit measures 13¾ inches high, 6½ inches deep, 4½ inches wide, has individual storage slots for 12 cartridges and is of the same sturdy construction and decorative appearance as the Cassette Case.

#J-8T12—4½" wide (holds 12 cartridges)
  $8.50 ea.
  3 for $23.50

#J-8T24—8½" wide (holds 24 cartridges)
  $10.95 ea.
  3 for $28.00

#J-8T36—12¾" wide (holds 36 cartridges)
  $14.25 ea.
  3 for $37.00

---

**Please send:**

| ITEM NO | COLOR (IF CHOICE) | DESCRIPTION | QUANTITY | UNIT PRICE | TOTAL COST |
|---------|-------------------|-------------|----------|------------|------------|
|         |                   |             |          |            |            |
|         |                   |             |          |            |            |
|         |                   |             |          |            |            |

Postage and handling charges (up to $10 add $1.50) ($10.01 to $20 add $2.50) ($20.01 to $40 add $3.50) (over $40 postage FREE)

I enclose ☐ check ☐ money order in amount of $ _____ Total _____

The New American Library, Inc.
P.O. Box 999
Bergenfield, New Jersey 07621

Name _____

Address _____

City _____ State _____ Zip _____

Offer valid only in the United States of America.    (Allow 5 weeks for delivery.)